DON CARLOS
INFANTE OF SPAIN

FRIEDRICH von SCHILLER

DON CARLOS

INFANTE OF SPAIN

A Drama in Five Acts

Translated by

CHARLES E. PASSAGE
Assistant Professor of World Literature
Brooklyn College

FREDERICK UNGAR PUBLISHING CO.
NEW YORK

Fifth Printing, 1980

ISBN 0-8044-6817-6

Copyright 1959 by Frederick Ungar Publishing Co.

Library of Congress Catalog Card Number 59-11672

Printed in the United States of America

INTRODUCTION

1. The Historical Facts about Don Carlos

On January 18, 1568 King Philip II of Spain, the most powerful of reigning monarchs in western Europe, attended Mass in the company of his only son and heir, Crown Prince Charles (Don Carlos). Apparent friendliness marked their meeting, though it was common knowledge that mutual and profound distrust had long prevailed between them. Shortly before midnight of the same day the King, attended by several of the highest noblemen of his court, presented himself suddenly and unexpectedly in his son's bedchamber and solemnly announced that as of that moment the bedchamber was to be his son's prison. The windows were nailed shut, all papers belonging to the Prince were confiscated, and guards were stationed at the door. A week later the prisoner was transferred to quarters still more secure, where orders still more stern were issued as precautions against his escape. Six months later, shortly after midnight of July 24, 1568, word was brought to the King that his son had died in his prison room. The age of the deceased was twenty-three years and sixteen days.

The six months of prison regime had been necessarily distressful, but neither physical comforts nor the consolations of religion had been denied. Under no circumstances had the Prince been allowed to leave confinement. A single high window afforded no view of the outside world. All messages were scrutinized by the King before delivery to the prisoner, and only spiritual books were permitted for his distraction. The particular quarters had been selected because they adjoined a chapel, but only through an iron grille could the Prince watch the sacrifice of the Mass and receive Holy Communion. His regular confessor visited him frequently. His jailer, Ruy Gomez, Prince of Eboli, performed his duties in all correctness. Servants brought unlimited quantities of food and of ice water, for the Prince drank no wine. The King never visited the prisoner.

From January until April Carlos apparently felt certain that pardon would sooner or later come from his father. On some days he raged against the tyrant until he was exhausted; his temper had always been phenomenal. Again he would eat himself into semi-stupor; his gluttony had often astonished the court; at one point he went to the opposite extreme and declared a hunger strike. When this was reported to the King, the latter remarked: "He will eat when hunger forces him to it." And so it was. Steadfastly, however, Carlos refused the sacraments, because he could not bring himself to abjure his hatred of his father. But it was the Easter season, and before the expiration of the season it was mandatory for a Catholic to receive the sacraments. His confessor was unable to resolve the issue, but a letter from an old friend, the jurist Dr. Suarez, at last brought him to the action for which the confessor had so long argued. Failure to confess his sins, including the hatred of his father, would preclude the receiving of Holy Communion, and failure to receive Holy Communion would mark him as a bad Catholic, unworthy ever to ascend the throne of Spain. Carlos was persuaded. He made his confession, renounced his hatred, and received at last through the iron grille the consecrated wafer. Then followed a period of spiritual calm marked by renewed hope of pardon and ultimate kingship. A few courtiers also felt the pardon must come sooner or later. But the King was inexorable. The heat of the summer began. The prisoner resorted anew to excesses of food and to excesses of ice water, alternating these excesses with unpredictable fasts. The physical collapse in mid-July seems to have been a ghastly dissolution of the digestive organs which had been taxed beyond endurance and now refused all function.

The King, meanwhile, was aware of the rumors in the city and in the court to the effect that Carlos had been imprisoned for inclinations toward Protestantism. It was an open secret that Carlos had recently planned flight from Spain and life abroad. For the most part, the monarch chose to disregard such talk, but to his Holy Father the Pope he deemed some explanation to be owing. A long royal explanation was accordingly drafted in May, in which Philip stated with insistence that he had not ordered his son's arrest in anger, nor for any particular "fault," nor by way of corrective punishment toward any specific objective; the arrest constituted protective custody of a prince whose intellectual and moral character made succession to the throne impossible beyond any conceivable doubt. The prisoner, he assured His Holiness, would have the best of treatment. The letter did not mention the King's abandoned intentions of either bringing Carlos to trial on some charge of treason or declaring him insane. Philip merely waited, and the end came sooner than anyone anticipated.

And once the end came, Philip ordered the utmost pomp and ceremony for his son's funeral. The highest grandees of Spain carried the coffin, the procession was accompanied by all foreign ambassadors, by the Austrian archdukes, by the Grand Inquisitor—but Philip himself viewed the procession from an upper-story window, and on the day of the actual interment he was absent in his palace of the Escurial.

What events, one may well ask, had brought about so desperate a mutual hatred? Things had not always been so between father and son. At the child's birth on July 8, 1545 the eighteen-year-old father had received the news with joy amid the imperial business that occupied him in the German city of Worms. A few days later there had come the unhappy word of the death of the young mother, Princess Maria of Portugal. Various persons of the royal family looked after the infant, always with divided authority, for neither the perennially travelling father nor the much occupied grand-father, the reigning Emperor Charles V, had time for atten-tion to a small boy. Both were, to be sure, delighted by their heir, and Philip in particular was all indulgence during the occasional periods when he had his son in his presence. Until age three the boy barely spoke at all, but once having ac-quired the art he seems to have lost no time in putting it to dubious use. By age five his temper tantrums were already rousing concern, and his earliest teachers collected some of the wittiest of the lad's sarcasms into a notebook for presen-tation to the Emperor. Between the lines of praise in their official reports to father and grandfather could be discerned traces of more realistic awareness that their charge was not learning as gloriously as their text asserted. By the time the Prince was thirteen they were being forced to admit that he was not learning at all. Moreover, Carlos was sickly, his complexion was bad, he was ungainly at sports.

From the archives of Venice there is extant the frank de-scription of the thirteen-year-old which was submitted by the Venetian ambassador to Spain to his home government. Carlos is haughty, brutal, intolerable; he practices loathe-some cruelty upon animals, such as roasting a rabbit alive; he is already a skirt-chaser; he is a reckless spendthrift; he claims he is interested solely in warfare, yet cannot handle weapons; he talks of *his* war and swears adult courtiers to follow *him* into that war; his specialty is the gratuitous insult to reverend elders. This startling report must to some degree be discounted: the Venetian ambassador was writing from Flanders, not from Spain, and on the hearsay of courtiers. Yet his successor, Paolo Tiepolo, who did know Carlos personally at age eighteen (1563), confirms and darkens the portrait. Carlos is undersized, ugly, physically weak, melancholy, dull in studies as in athletics, ill-tempered, vicious and vindictive; his slow speech consists of interminable questions punctuated by gross insults to all and sundry—even his father. St. Sulpice, the French ambassador, actually speaks of "imbécilité." Don Chaves, life-long confessor to the Prince, declares that his youthful charge is not insane, but the word "devilish" recurs more than once in his description; on the whole, however, Don Chaves maintains that the Prince talks more evilly than he acts.

Less damning, though not entirely reassuring, is the description of another eyewitness, Baron von Dietrichstein. Carlos, he says, has good facial features, brown hair, a low forehead, a long chin; he is small of build, with one shoulder higher than the other and with a right leg shorter than the left; his voice is high pitched, his speech slow, with a tendency to confuse "l" and "r." The Baron mentions the temper displays but puts them down to bad upbringing; he mentions the incessant questions but finds them often quite sensible; he mentions the sharp remarks but finds them the fearless, almost naive statements of the bitter truth. The Baron then goes on to praise Carlos's excellent memory, his genuine piety, his love of all honest people, his generosity. He even pleads extenuation in the antagonism of the youth's father and in the aggravating assignment of bad servants to his retinue.

At some early point the father-son antipathy began. Upon the publication of a courtier's pompous book of description of King Philip's journey to the Netherlands to receive the homage of the Low German princes, it was a teen-age Carlos who circulated a blank notebook entitled "The Great and Wondrous Journeys of the King Don Philip'" and with chapter headings: "The Journey from Madrid to the Park in Segovia," "From the Park in Segovia to the Escurial," "From the Escurial to Aranjuez," "From Aranjuez to the Escurial," etc. Upon discovering the satire the humorless King and father could not adequately express his rage. At a still earlier age a grotesquely puerile Carlos had declared he would challenge to a duel any half brother his father might beget upon his second wife, Queen Mary Tudor of England, especially if the half brother were to inherit any part of the Spanish empire. No half brother was begotten, nor did Carlos ever meet this stepmother who died in 1558, but he did meet and cherish a personal fondness for his father's third wife, the French Princess Elizabeth de Valois, the Queen in Schiller's drama. She was, in fact, one of the very few gentlewomen at court whom he did not insult. His confiscated papers brought to light a list of "Friends" with the Queen's name at the head of the list—also a list of "Enemies" with his father's name at the head of the list—but there is not the slightest suggestion of an erotic connection between the two. Elizabeth survived Carlos's death by only three months, but this fact seems to have been pure coincidence. As for his father's amours at court, Carlos seems to have loathed them, and had none of his own. For himself, he chose public harlots, whom he visited with troops of raucous cronies, yet he was wont to speak with rapture of marriage with Mary Queen of Scots or with his cousin, the Princess Anne of Austria, neither of whom he ever saw. Marriage with the Scottish Queen was briefly but never very seriously considered by the King and his advisors, but marriage with Anne was repeatedly urged by the Austrian house and repeatedly postponed by Philip over a period of years. After the death of his son and third wife Philip himself married the Princess Anne.

It was at a tryst with a castellan's daughter in Alcalá that Carlos suffered a grievous fall down a flight of stairs on April 19, 1562. Besides a severe head injury, a high fever developed and the young man was not expected to live. Philip rather over-hastily issued instructions for a funeral and left his son. But a famous Dutch surgeon performed a trepanning operation on the skull and the patient recovered. The Prince always attributed his recovery to the prayers of a monk who was reputed to be a saint.

By rights, the Crown Prince should have been presented to the various component states of Spain to receive their homage. In 1552 Philip had presented his seven-year-old son in Castile, but to Aragon, Valencia, and Catalonia the presentation was never made. At a convocation of the estates of Aragon in the summer of 1563 there were several months of opportunity, but Philip alleged that Carlos was ill and unable to appear. At some point between those dates the father had made up his mind that Carlos was unfit to reign. In 1564 the King openly spoke of the Austrian Archdukes Matthias and Ernst as his heirs. Nothing in the Prince's health or behavior suggested that his father's aversion deserved to be reassured, though grudging permission was granted the youth to preside over meetings of the State Council. Thus the King may have welcomed the news brought to him during his weeks of ascetic seclusion in the Escurial for the Christmas season of 1567. First, it reached the King's ears that on December 27th Carlos had called together some sixteen learned monks to inquire of them whether he could receive absolution in Confession without renouncing his hatred for a certain person. His confessor had already refused such absolution, and without it Carlos could not receive Holy Communion on the occasion of the Jubilee Indulgence recently proclaimed by Pope Pius V, when all Spain would be receiving the Sacrament. When the monks concurred with the decision of the confessor, the Prince had then asked to be allowed to receive an unconsecrated Host, but this too had been rejected as an act of sacrilege. That the Prince had spoken not only of implacable hatred but also of intended murder of a certain person is almost certainly a distortion of his confessor's report, since the confessor later stated that Carlos had never planned any act of violence. Next, it was reliably reported to the King that Carlos was making urgent efforts to raise 600,000 ducats in cash; that he had composed letters protesting his father's cruel treatment and sent them to the Pope, to all Catholic monarchs of Europe, to all the estates of Spain; that he had tried to persuade his father's illegitimate half brother, Don Juan of Austria, as Admiral of the Spanish navy, to furnish him with a ship, promising him the gift of either Naples or Milan as reward. Flight abroad was clearly indicated, and to the King only rebellion and treason were believable motives. It is quite possible, however, that the motives were those of an aggrieved son who took no thought of what such actions would entail, who, indeed, would not have been able to grasp their grave political implications for Spain and Europe.

The information was all in the King's possession by December 28, 1567. Still in retreat at the Escurial, the King ordered prayers to be said beginning January 12, 1568 for his divine guidance in serious decisions. On January 17th he returned to Madrid. On the morning of the 18th he attended Mass in the company of his son. That same evening he proclaimed his son's arrest.

II. From History to Legend

In Spain these unbeautiful facts were remembered in Cabrera's *Historia de Felipe Segundo, Rey de España* (1619) and in at least three native dramas drawn from that work in the course of the seventeenth century. The *interpretation of the facts* was that of the officially inspired rumors which could have originated only with Philip himself: Carlos was feebleminded, possibly even insane; he harbored notions of Protestant heresy; his plan of flight betokened outright treason, specifically alliance with the Netherlands rebels; he died of overeating, but he died repentant and a loyal Catholic.

Elsewhere the facts endured a sea change, to emerge as the *legend* of Don Carlos, which, in defiance of actuality, set a Prince of youthful grace and charm amid the events and made of him a pathetic martyr to love and to political idealism .

Gossip attributed Protestant leanings to Carlos even while he was still alive, and even the irate father assumed that the destination of his son's projected flight was the rebellious Netherlands. As early as 1570 Protestant exiles from the Low Countries presented to Emperor Maximilian II a formal protest of Carlos's arrest, imprisonment, and *execution by the Inquisition* for having favored the Dutch and Flemish cause. It seems to have been William of Orange who first made a sinister connection between the death of Carlos and the death of his stepmother Elizabeth three months later: Philip must have killed them both in order to marry his son's fiancée, Anne of Austria, himself. At the time of the ambiguous Protestant triumph in France in 1593, when Henri IV embraced the Catholic faith in order to conclude four years of civil war and become the acknowledged king of that country, one Antonio Perez, a renegade Spaniard, made a statement to a member of the Paris Parlement to the effect that Philip had denounced his son to the Inquisition out of *jealousy for his son's attachment to the Queen* and out of horror at his treasonable sympathy with the Netherlands; the Inquisition had then effected the young man's death by slow doses of poisoned food over a period of four months. In his *Relaciones* of 1598 Perez embroidered the tale with horrendous incidents, such as the furious attempt of the Prince of Eboli, Carlos's jailer, to strangle Don Chaves, Carlos's confessor, because he revolted at the vile priest's slow murder of the victim. Another tributary enters the stream of legend in the form of the memoirs of Pierre de Bourdeille, Abbé de Brantôme, who had observed Carlos personally in 1564 in Madrid and from that period recalled ugly truths about the Prince's scandalous behavior toward women in the city streets and unnatural cruelties, for example, Carlos's forcing a luckless cobbler to cut up and eat an ill-made pair of shoes. Later, however, under Protestant influence, Brantôme tended to see the Prince as a political idealist and *friend of Count Egmont,* a believer in religious toleration and Dutch independence, and *betrayed by the Princess Eboli.* The edition of Brantôme's *Vies des grands capitaines,* published 1665-1666 *in Leyden,* enjoyed great popularity in non-Spanish Europe, a popularity that continued long, as attested by reprints in 1740, 1779, 1787, and 1790.

In 1672 the legend received definitive form at the hands of the French romancer and pseudo-historian, César Vichard Saint-Réal, whose eighty-page *Dom Carlos, Nouvelle Historique* is elaborately footnoted with references to "manuscript as well as printed works" from "all the Spanish, French, Italian, and Flemish authors who have written about the era." Yet the opening words of the preface strike the tone of romance at once:

"Tous les Historiens du siècle passé qui parlent du malheureux Prince d'Espagne qui fait le sujet de cet Ouvrage, parlent aussi de son amour pour sa belle-mère."

Deftly the account begins with the bethrothal of Carlos and Elizabeth after Carlos has seen a portrait of the Princess. A succinct account of war, truce, and the entry to power of new diplomats quickly reverses the state of affairs to make Elizabeth the affianced bride of the father instead of the son. Carlos arrives at the French border to escort the Princess to Madrid, and in the carriage ensues a scene of tender glances exchanged between the young people. At the end of the journey Elizabeth casts another significant glance at her husband-to-be: Was she looking to see whether his hair was gray? Once at court, the dutiful bride incurs the jealousy of the "irregularly" beautiful Princess of Eboli, who, defeated now in her amatory designs upon the King, will turn her attention to the Prince. Enter at this point Don Juan of Austria, the King's illegitimate half brother, who falls in love with Elizabeth himself. When his love is not returned he has recourse to a series of stratagems to determine whether he is right in suspecting that Carlos and Elizabeth are cherishing an adulterous passion behind his half brother's back. His stratagems fail with Carlos, fail with Elizabeth, and so he enlists the aid of the Princess Eboli to work the young people's ruin. The narrative digresses for a time to deal with Count Egmont's visit, his friendship with Carlos, and Carlos's politically and religiously liberal inclinations. One day Carlos sustains an injury when his horse—a gift to him from the citizens of the town of Alcalá—runs away with him. "Le Marquis de Posa, son favori" is despatched to inform the Queen that the Prince has been mortally injured. The

Princess of Eboli is present to witness the Queen's profound agitation at the news. Meanwhile the King has conceived the suspicion that his young wife is secretly in love with the Marquis Posa, especially after the Marquis wears her colors in a joust. The new suspicion creates a dilemma. Carlos and Posa cannot both be her lovers; one must be the lover, the other the lover's confidant. Ruy Gomez, Prince of Eboli, is summoned to discuss with the King measures for having Posa murdered. Suddenly the King shifts direction, orders the arrest of Carlos, and submits his correspondence, minus the letters to the Queen, to the Inquisition. The doomed Prince is allowed to avoid death from slow poison by opening his veins in a hot bath. He dies contemplating the same locket picture of the Queen with which the story began. Hurried statements add that Spanish historians have falsified these facts to flatter the tyrant, that Elizabeth died soon afterward, that the Count of Lerma attended Carlos faithfully in those last days, and that the Princess Eboli was imprisoned for having forged the letters that incriminated Carlos before the Inquisition.

III. From Saint-Réal to Schiller

The French romancer's idealist-martyr to love and liberty found immediate sympathy with readers of that and subsequent days, and Saint-Réal's book, in the French original, in four German translations, and in two English translations, was to provide the source material for a whole series of creative writers in different countries and in significantly different generations. In the form "Englished by H. J." in London, 1676, Thomas Otway discovered the substance of his resounding tragedy in heroic couplets entitled *Don Carlos, Prince of Spain* (1676), in which the emotional coloring is labored to resemble Shakespeare's *Othello*. In Germany, poets drew on Saint-Réal for grandiose Baroque "heroic epistles" (Heldenbriefe): Daniel Casper von Lohenstein in his hundred-line *König Philipp an die Fürstin Eboly* and its hundred-line counterpart, *Eboly an den König Philippen,* and "Philander van der Linde" (Johann Burkhard Mencke) in his *Liebe zwischen Carl dem Infanten von Spanien und seiner Stiefmutter Isabella.* In Saint-Réal's own country one Jean Galbert de Campistron transposed the matter and the characters to Byzantium and, substituting Greeks and Bulgars for Spaniards and Flemish, retold the pathetic story in the form of a classical tragedy named for its Carlos-hero *Andronic* (1685).

These latter seventeenth-century plays and poems conceived of the tale as an approximation of Greek and Roman sublimity. The essence of the fable was the tragic conflict between love and duty on the princely plane, a theme which the age considered the ultimate in poignancy and nobility. With the waning of the Baroque age the theme lapsed from favor, and for more than fifty years no poets were attracted to it. The Dutch reprints of Saint-Réal's romance during this interval—1722 and 1724 in The Hague and 1740 in Amsterdam—are doubtless to be explained in terms of Dutch patriotism.

But with the new era of Rousseau the Don Carlos story enjoyed a popular revival. The two German translations of Otway's play in 1757 and 1770 may reflect only the general interest in English literature. In 1774, however, the Italian dramatist Vittorio Alfieri presented a drama, written in French, on the subject, and two years later, in 1776, made his own Italian version of the same work under the title of *Filippo II*. It was the hero of this drama that Carlyle identified as "perhaps the most wicked man that human imagination has conceived." In 1781 a French Don Carlos tragedy, originally called *Elizabeth de France,* was banned by the government, but within two years its now forgotten author, Pierre Lefèvre, succeeded in getting it performed at the theatre of the Duc d'Orléans. An Italian tragedy on the same subject, by one Alessandro Pepoli, bears the publication date of "Naples, 1784." Two historical treatments in prose appeared side by side with these dramatic versions. Schiller is known to have made use of the German translation of Robert Watson's *History of the Reign of Philip II* (Lübeck, 1778), and he made his own translation of Louis-Sébastien Mercier's *Portrait de Philippe second* (1785) and appended it to the text of his play as the latter appeared in the *Thalia* magazine in 1786.

As the culmination of these predominantly sentimental or liberal Don Carlos works stands Schiller's justly famous sentimental and liberal drama, *Don Carlos, Infant von Spanien,* completed in its blank verse form in 1787.

IV. From Schiller to Verdi

Schiller's drama totally eclipsed all predecessors, including Saint-Réal's long-admired romance, and by its immense popularity through the nineteenth century provided the point of departure for all subsequent treatments of the theme.

Alongside more than twenty-five translations into various European languages—twelve of them into English—stand almost as many stage adaptations of the over-long German text, varying from moderately faithful to extremely free. One of these is the hapless version of William Dunlap which received a single performance in New York at the Park Theatre on May 6, 1799. Three British adaptations were made in the 1820's. Bayard Taylor left a version in manuscript, dated 1877. In the season of 1905-1906 Richard Mansfield toured the United States with a stage version based on the translation by the Englishman R. D. Boylan of 1847. Paris saw two French acting versions in 1848 and in 1855.

Over-familiarity with the play prompted various parodies. One of them by Ludwig Tieck was conceived as a private joke for his daughter's birthday party in either 1807 or 1808, but in 1851-52 one Silvius Landsberger regaled the German public with more than a hundred performances of *Don Carlos, Infantryman of Spain, or What comes of being in love with your mother-in-law* (Don Carlos, der Infanterist von Spanien, oder das kommt davon, wenn man seine Schwiegermutter liebt). An anonymous mid-century German produced *Don Carlos with the Barnstormers* (Don Carlos auf der Schmiere), while in 1869 the London vaudeville audiences were amused by Conway Edwardes' *Don Carlos; or, The Infant in Arms.*

Serious writers of the same period found inspiration in the play. Byron's 586-line poem *Parisina* (1816) represents a variant of the plot. Fouqué's romantic drama *Don Carlos, Infant von Spanien* (1823) is dedicated to Schiller. Grillparzer's early work *Blanka von Castilien* patently echoes Schiller's play and betokens the strong Schillerian strain in Grillparzer's whole career. Two serious operatic versions antedate Verdi's great one, a *Don Carlos* by M. Costa (London, 1844) and a *Don Carlos* by Vincenzo Moscuzza (Naples, 1862).

Wide interest in Schiller's drama inevitably raised questions about the historical facts involved, and although scholarly treatment had already been accorded the subject by the previously mentioned Watson and Mercier prior to 1787, a whole new line of historians becomes involved in the study after 1829. The line is initiated in that year by the famous Leopold von Ranke, whose sketch entitled *Zur Geschichte des Don Carlos* was the first to strive for dispassionate objectivity and the first to base itself on a significant number of documents assembled from the historical period in question. Rejecting the love story as sheer invention and rejecting the charges of patricide and rebellion as untenable exaggerations, Ranke saw the story as a psychological case of father-son hatred. He also recognized what must be recognized by any artist, historian, or psychologist who seeks to deal seriously with the matter, that the issue depends much more on the character of Philip than on the character of Carlos. Amplifications of Ranke's sketch followed from the pens of Friedrich von Raumer (1831), Matthias Koch (1857), the famous American historian William Prescott (1855), and the Spaniard Modesto Lafuente (1854), and their collective interpretations, generally hostile to Philip and favorable to Carlos, were consolidated in the major work, *Don Carlos et Philippe II*, 1863, by the Belgian scholar Gachard, who tended to see Philip in even darker colors still. The very next year, 1864, witnessed the arrival on the scene of a scholarly opponent, Maurenbrecher, who five years later, in 1869, published a much enlarged book which portrayed Carlos as a dangerous semi-lunatic and Philip as a distressed monarch compelled to carry out a harsh but necessary duty. The study published by Schmidt in 1874 revived the old arch-Protestant interpretation of a tyrant father and a liberal Crown Prince, the latter caught in cunning nets of the former's contriving and "in all probability" poisoned. With three recent opinions from scientific historians in conflict a "Don Carlos controversy" in the academic world was inevitable. The controversy rose, and it raged for another fifty years. It has never been finally settled and it is unlikely that it ever will be settled in a manner that will satisfy all parties concerned. We have chosen here to follow the guidance of Professor Felix Rachfahl, whose *Don Carlos. Kritische Untersuchungen* of 1921 seemed to us a soberly reasonable book. Apart from the discovery of new documentation, however, the meagre facts and the gaudy rumors are all before us and their exact meaning will necessarily vary from reader to reader.

There remains to speak of the opera which Verdi created for the Paris audiences at the time of the Exposition of 1867. Two librettists, Joseph Méry and Camille Du Locle, had prepared a long text in French, the opening scene of which presented the young lovers Carlos and Elizabeth in the idyllic forest of Fontainebleau. A number of years later, after composing *Aïda* and *Otello,* Verdi reworked the score on the basis of a shorter Italian text prepared by Boïto. This four-act version begins and ends in the Monastery of St. Just with the tomb of the great Emperor Charles V visible at the left of the stage. Carlos, entering, listens to a chorus of monks singing of the insignificance of human glory and is briefly accosted by a lone monk who has been praying before the tomb. As the latter disappears Carlos believes he recognizes his grandfather's, the great Emperor's, voice. Charles V did, after his abdication in 1556, retire to a monastery, but Carlos was only eleven years old at the time. In the final scene of the opera Philip and the Inquisitors and courtiers emerge from the shadows of this same chapel to seize the doomed hero, but at precisely that moment the Emperor Charles V in full regalia confronts them, himself advancing from the shadows around the tomb. Whether a ghost or the actual Emperor living beyond his recorded death in 1558, is not said, but as the curtain falls he takes Carlos with him and the King and the Inquisitor stand appalled by what they have witnessed. The librettists have clearly availed them-selves of hints contained in lines 5112-5136 of the German text in order to make a kind of closed frame around the action of the opera as a whole. Their further changes were largely in the reordering of scenes and parts of scenes and in the heavy task of cutting the text to libretto length. On the whole they remained very faithful to their source work and nothing essential was allowed to be lost. To this skillful adaptation Verdi added his incomparable music, so that this extraordinary combination of the youthful Schiller and the aged Verdi emerges as one of the most overwhelmingly great works in operatic literature, the nineteenth-century equivalent of the late eighteenth-century drama of idealism.

From sixteenth-century arresting facts to tragic courtly romance in the seventeenth century, thence to memorable drama of an idealist's martyrdom in 1787, and on to mighty music drama in the nineteenth century; from facts of the Spanish court to French romancer's grace, thence to a German's impassioned plea for love and liberty, and on to an Italian's exaltation in song; through eras of changing taste, through utter reversal of political organizations, the Don Carlos story remains inexhaustibly fascinating. Surely the twentieth century will not close without some new version that will cast fresh light into its persistent mystery.

Meanwhile Schiller's drama will remain a noble monument to the human mind in its own right, enduringly profound on its own merits and by no means lost in a bygone age.

V. Schiller's *Don Carlos*

The source for Schiller's work was Saint-Réal's romance, with subsidiary details added from Robert Watson's *History of the Reign of Philip II* in the German translation of 1778, and attempts of scholars to demonstrate that Schiller consulted and consolidated the numerous literary versions of his predecessors remain inconclusive. The subject first attracted his attention in 1782, after completion of his first play, *The Robbers* (Die Räuber, published May, 1781), and while at work on his second play, *Fiesco* (published 1783). Born November 10, 1759, he had just passed the age of twenty-three years and sixteen days, the age at which Don Carlos died, when in the spring of 1783 he drew up his first outline for his drama on the Spanish subject, the so-called "Bauerbach Sketch," a terse memorandum of a few pages, partly in phrase form, and arranged in five "Steps." Don Juan of Austria is here assigned a role, as might be expected in a dramatization of Saint-Réal, but we also find a note to the effect that "the Marquis" diverts suspicion to himself; the last two items under "Step V" read as follows:

"C. The testimony of the dying woman and the crime of the accusers justify the Prince too late.
D. Grief of the betrayed King and vengeance on the perpetrators."

From April 3, 1783 dates also a letter to Dalberg, the director of the National Theatre in Mannheim and the person who had first suggested the theme to him, stating that he is already working on this "fruitful" subject. The work lapsed for a time, however, while *Kabale und Liebe,* originally entitled for its heroine *Luise Müllerin,* was being completed and published in 1784. By the end of 1784 the youthful author was able to give a reading in Darmstadt of the first act of "Dom Carlos" (Saint-Réal's spelling!) in the presence of Duke Karl August of Weimar, as a reward for which the Duke conferred upon him the title of Weimar Councillor.

This lone act, composed in prose, was published in March 1785 in the first and only issue of the magazine, *Rheinische Thalia,* that ever appeared, though its successor, the *Thalia,* was to carry the text of Act II and part of Act III (to line 2940 of the present version) in irregular installments from 1785 to 1787. By that time the initial prose draft had been converted into the new medium of blank verse, which Les-sing had first used in an important work in *Nathan the Wise* (1779). With 4140 lines of text already before the public, constituting a little more than half of the projected total, the author now found himself committed to courses of action which he would gladly have altered. Now it was apparent to him that the Marquis Posa was a far more profound and significant personage than he himself had realized, and, unable to change what he had already published, he continued to write as poetic inspiration dictated, thus forcing himself to invent more and more elaborate explanations of how the new action squared with the old.

The end product was a "dramatic poem" of 6,282 lines with a plot so bewilderingly involved that Schiller himself sought to explain its evolution and meaning in a series of essays known as the *Letters on Don Carlos* (Briefe über Don Carlos), published in the *Deutscher Merkur* from July to December of 1788. For an edition of the play that appeared in 1801 the author reduced the total number of lines from 6,282 to 5,448. Just before his death he supervised the edition of 1805 which further cut the text to 5,370 lines. It is this final version which is given in the present translation. Even so, the drama has the length of almost any two plays of Shakespeare put together and two-thirds the length of Schiller's own trilogy of plays on the subject of Wallenstein.

The play as it stands is much too long. Its plot is snarled with intricacies and its motivations are not always clear. Too often it withholds vital secrets from the audience, it relies on coincidence overfrequently, it indulges and overindulges in the mannerism of crucially important documents held in the characters' hands but which the audience or reader is not permitted to examine. Its rhetoric sometimes drowns the action in words. Its faults lie exposed where the dullest viewer catches sight of them at once, faults which any literary hack could disguise or obviate altogether. Indeed, two very obscure Frenchmen did so rearrange and shorten the work as to make an opera libretto for Verdi that is far more concise and clear than the German original. But who, other than Schiller, could have conceived the great scenes? Where, in all of literature, is there a play that, by sheer force and grandeur, lives down faults as gross as this play does? The fifth act alone staggers the imagination, and its penultimate scene, that with the Grand Inquisitor, as the creation of a young man in his middle twenties, is nothing short of astounding. It arrests the attention of any reader today; it evoked from Verdi the astonishing achievement of matching it in music; it evoked from Dostoevski the famous rival scene of the Grand Inquisitor in *The Brothers Karamazov*.

Adequate discussion of the work would require a volume, and only very general comments can be made here. Any father-son conflict resulting in the destruction of the life of the younger by the older man is at once poignant to the highest intensity. When the father is a King and the son a Crown Prince on whom future destinies depend throughout an empire, the poignancy is multiplied tenfold. Neither Schiller nor his contemporaries could have been unaware that something very like this story had occurred within the memory of living persons in the case of Frederick the Great of Prussia and his father Frederick William I, except that the son in that instance survived and reigned. Some persons may well have recalled that earlier in the same century Peter the Great of Russia had slain his son and heir under circumstances not too different from those of Philip and Carlos. These parallels are no doubt coincidental. But with the entrance into the equation of the second young man, the Posa-type, the problem becomes more complex. A set of literary parallels suggests itself at once: Carlos-Hamlet, Philip-Claudius, Posa-Horatio. Alternately, Carlos-Hamlet,

Philip-Claudius, Posa-Laertes, with all the tensions that derive from a situation where the King-father finds his own son repugnant as human being and as heir but finds the stranger-youth wholly worthy. Further parallels with *Hamlet* confirm the former ones: the respective Queens and ambiguous mothers, Elizabeth and Gertrude; the well-intentioned but meddlesome old men and trusted friends to the throne, Lerma and Polonius; even Don Luis Mercado and Osric perform parallel dramatic functions in their brief single scenes at parallel points in the drama; and the rumor of Charles V's regal ghost unmistakeably recalls the majestic ghost of Hamlet's father. A major aesthetic consideration in the assessment of Schiller's creation consists of realizing that he saw Saint-Réal's romance through the prism of Shakespeare's *Hamlet*. Such juxtaposition accounts in no small measure for the intensity of the final work. But behind the trio of Philip-Carlos-Posa stands another trio also, lending still greater power to the already fiercely charged matter, namely, the trio of Saul-David-Jonathan. The Grand Inquisitor scene testifies to the Biblical parallel, and lines 5251 ff. refer specifically to the first Book of Samuel. A certain love-rivalry seems all but inescapable here, and Thomas Mann chose *Don Carlos* as precisely the right book to have young Tonio Kröger urge upon his friend Hans Hansen. To all these elements must be added the furious clash of ideologies, both political and religious, amid which the tragedy is fulfilled. Schiller's radiant passion for liberty transfigures the personal tragedy with the white light of martyrdom and the rainbow promise of better ages to come for all mankind. What autobiographical experiences underlie the entire nexus of powerful emotions are mostly beyond our valid control, but it may be mentioned as not unimportant that the young author had known a harsh father and a tyrant Duke in real life and that he had had at least two dedicated friendships before undertaking this drama.

From the totality of characters and action looms up the figure of the King with larger than human size, for Schiller rightly saw that the crux of the story was the father rather than the son. Not that the play is mistitled: Carlos is the center of the plot. But his hopeless conflicts are mitigated by the assurance of the Queen's love and by the ultimate sacrifice of Posa for his sake. Moreover, his conflicts end in death. Philip, on the other hand, must go on living, living without love, conscience-haunted, and defeated. With his young wife he failed, as he failed with his mistress; with his adopted son Posa he failed, as he failed with his own son; he failed in human friendship; he failed as King, for the ultimate power is the Grand Inquisitor's, whose puppet he must be. And he has no heir. Henceforth he must exist in a ghastly cage of pomp without substance, amid evil memories. Worst of all, he has, as his tears revealed, the capacity to feel these things to the full of their horror. It is true that his feelings have all been converted by the end of the drama into the single emotion of hate. But he hates as a mighty fallen angel hates who broods in outer darkness remembering God's light.

Schiller was to write a technically much superior work, *Wallenstein,* as his next composition ten years later, but the paradox is that out of the clumsy faults and shortcomings of *Don Carlos* emerge his most unforgettably tremendous characters. Nothing in German drama can match the sombre grandeur of this play.

DON CARLOS
INFANTE OF SPAIN

CHARACTERS

PHILIP II, King of Spain
ELIZABETH OF VALOIS, his spouse
DON CARLOS, the Crown Prince
ALEXANDER FARNESE, PRINCE OF PARMA, nephew of the King
INFANTA CLARA EUGENIA, a child of three years
DUCHESS OF OLIVAREZ, chief stewardess
MARQUISE OF MONDECAR ⎫
PRINCESS OF EBOLI   ⎬ Ladies to the Queen
COUNTESS FUENTES   ⎭
MARQUIS OF POSA, a Knight of Malta ⎫
DUKE OF ALBA   ⎪
COUNT OF LERMA, chief of the bodyguard   ⎬ Grandees of
DUKE OF FERIA, Knight of the Golden Fleece ⎪ Spain
DUKE OF MEDINA SIDONIA, Admiral   ⎪
DON RAIMOND OF TAXIS, Chief Postmaster ⎭
DOMINGO, the King's confessor
THE GRAND INQUISITOR of the realm
THE PRIOR of a Carthusian monastery
A PAGE of the Queen
DON LUIS MERCADO, the Queen's physician

Various ladies and grandees, pages, officers, the bodyguard,
        and persons with non-speaking parts

Time: Spring, 1568

ACT I

The royal garden in Aranjuez.
Carlos. Domingo.

DOMINGO: The lovely days here in Aranjuez
    Have come now to a close. Your Royal Highness does
    Not leave this place more cheerful than he came.
    We have spent time for nothing here. Break off
    This riddling silence. Open up your heart
    Unto your father's heart, Prince. Never can
    The monarch buy too dearly his son's peace—
    His only son's.—No price can be too high.
         (Carlos stares at the ground in silence.)
    Can some wish be still unfulfilled which Heaven
    Has yet denied the dearest of its sons?   10
    I too was there, when in Toledo's walls
    Proud Charles received the homage rendered him,
    When princes forward thronged to kiss his hand,
    And now in one—one single low prostration—
    Six realms of kings bowed down before his feet.
    I stood and watched the proud and youthful blood
    Surge up within his cheeks, and watched his bosom
    Seethe with its princely resolutions, saw
    His eye exultant dart across the assembly,
    And then grow dim with rapture.—Prince, that eye   20
    Acknowledged: "I am satisfied."
         (Carlos turns away.)
              This silent
    And solemn sorrow, Prince, which we have read

3

These eight months now upon your countenance,
The riddle of this entire court, the anguish
Of this whole kingdom, has already cost
His Majesty so many care-worn nights
And cost your mother many tears.

CARLOS: *(turning around swiftly)*   My mother?—
O Heaven, grant I may forget his action
Who caused her to become my mother!

DOMINGO: Prince?

CARLOS: *(reflecting and passing his hand over his forehead)*
Reverend Sir,—I have had very much   30
Misfortune with my mothers. My first action
When I beheld the light of this world was
A mother's murder.

DOMINGO: Is it possible,
Dear Prince? Can this reproach be weighing on
Your conscience?

CARLOS: And my newest mother, has
She not cost me my father's love already?
My father scarcely loved me. My whole merit
Lay in the fact I was his only son.
Now she has given him a daughter.—Who
Knows what yet slumbers in the depths of time?   40

DOMINGO: You mock me, Prince. All Spain adores its Queen.
Could you then be the only one to gaze
Upon her with the eyes of hatred? Or
Hear only subtlety when gazing at her?
What, Prince? The fairest woman in the world—
And Queen—and once your own affianced bride?
Impossible! Incredible, Prince! Never!
When all else love, Charles cannot hate alone;
Thus oddly Carlos will not contradict
His nature. Take heed, Prince, she never learn   50
Of how displeased her son may be in her.
Report of it would cause her pain.

CARLOS: You think so?

DOMINGO: If Your Highness still recalls the recent
  Tournament in Saragossa when
  Our sovereign was grazed by a splintered lance,—
  The Queen was sitting with her ladies on
  The middle tier of seats before the palace
  Watching the contest. Suddenly the cry
  Went up: "The King is wounded!"—People throng
  Pell-mell, a muffled murmur carries to   60
  The Queen's own ear. "The Prince?" she cries, and starts to—
  And starts to rush down from the upper tier.
  "No!" comes the answer, "No! the King himself!"
  "In that case let them send for surgeons!" she
  Replies, and meanwhile sought to catch her breath.
         (*after a certain silence*)
  You stand, then, lost in thought?

CARLOS: I marvel at
  So jolly a confessor of the King,
  And one so versed in witty anecdotes.
         (*seriously and sombrely*)
  However, I have always heard it said
  That tattle-bearers and expression-watchers   70
  Have caused more evil in this world than poison
  Or daggers ever could in murderers' hands.
  You might have spared yourself the trouble. If
  It's thanks you're looking for, go to the King.

DOMINGO: You do well, Prince, to be thus on your guard
  With people—with discrimination. Do not
  Reject alike the friend and the deceiver.
  I speak in your best interests.

CARLOS: Then do
  Not let my father notice it. Or else
  You'll never get your purple.

DOMINGO: (*startled*)   What?

CARLOS: Why, yes.   80
  Did he not promise the first purple to you
  That would be Spain's to give?

DOMINGO: You mock me, Prince.

CARLOS: Now God forbid that I should mock the man,
  The awe-inspiring man who can pronounce
  My father blessed or declare him damned.

DOMINGO: Prince, I shall not be so presumptuous
  As to force my way into the solemn
  Secret of your sorrow. But I beg
  Your Highness to be mindful of the fact
  That for tormented consciences the church   90
  Has opened an asylum to which monarchs
  Themselves do not possess the key of entry,
  Where even criminal misdeeds lie stored
  Away beneath the sacramental seal.—
  You understand, Prince, what I mean.—I have
  Said quite enough.

CARLOS: No, no! Far be it from
  Me thus to tempt the keeper of the seal!

DOMINGO: Prince, this mistrust—You are misjudging your
  Most faithful servant.

CARLOS: (*takes him by the hand.*) Then you would do better
  To give me up. You are a holy man,   100
  The world is well aware of that,—but frankly,
  For me you are already over-taxed.
  Your road is very lengthy, reverend Father,
  Before you come to sit in Peter's chair.
  Much knowledge might weigh you unduly down.
  Report this to the King who sent you here.

DOMINGO: Who sent me here—

CARLOS: Those were my words. O yes,
  Too well, too well I know that at this court
  I am betrayed.—I know a hundred eyes
  Have been engaged to spy on me. I know   110
  King Philip has sold off his only son
  Into his basest henchmen's hands, and that
  My every uttered syllable is paid for
  With a more princely price to the informer

Than he has ever paid for any *good* deed.
I know—Be still! No more of that. My heart
Is on the verge of overflowing, and
I have already said too much.
DOMINGO: The King
Intends to reach Madrid before the evening.
The Court already is assembling. Have I   120
Permission, Prince,—
CARLOS: Quite. I will follow you.
                    (*Exit Domingo. After a pause*)
Unhappy Philip, like your son, unhappy!
I see your soul already bleeding from
Suspicion's venomed serpent-sting, and your
Disastrous curiosity hastes toward
The fearfulest of all discoveries,
And you will writhe, once you have come upon it.
                    (*Enter the Marquis of Posa.*)
Who comes?—What do I see? O blessed spirits!
My Roderick!
MARQUIS: My Carlos!
CARLOS: Can this be?
Can it be true? Can it be really you?—   130
It is! I press you to my soul, I feel
Yours beat almightily against my own.
O, everything is well now once again.
In this embrace my ailing heart is healed.
I lie upon my Roderick's neck.
MARQUIS: Your ailing—
Your ailing heart? And what is well again?
What was it needed making well again?
What you say startles me.
CARLOS: And what brings you
Back here so unexpectedly from Brussels?
Whom should I thank for this surprise? Whom? I   140
Still ask? Forgive, O Providence sublime,
The joy-delirious man this blasphemy!

Whom else but you, O All-benevolent?
You knew Don Carlos lacked an angel, you
Have sent me this one, and I go on asking.
MARQUIS: Forgive me, my dear Prince, if I now meet
This stormy rapture only with dismay.
It was not thus that I expected to
Behold Don Philip's son. Unnatural red   150
On your pale cheeks is kindled, and your lips
Are quivering as with fever. What am I
To think, dear Prince?—This is not that bold youth
Of lion's courage to whom I am sent
By a heroic people in suppression.—
For I do not stand here as Roderick now,
Nor as the playmate of the boy-Prince Carlos,—
As deputy of all humanity
I now embrace you,—and it is the Flemish
Provinces that weep upon your neck
And solemnly cry out to you for rescue.   160
That land so dear to you is lost if Alba,
The brutal hangman of Fanaticism,
Moves into Brussels with his Spanish laws.
With Emperor Charles's glorious grandson rests
The last hope of those noble provinces.
It will collapse if his sublime heart has
Forgotten how to beat for human kind.
CARLOS: It will collapse.
MARQUIS: Alas! What do I hear!
CARLOS: You speak of times that are now past and done.
I too once dreamed about a Charles into   170
Whose cheeks a fire would leap when discourse ran
On freedom.—That one long ago was buried.
The Charles you see here is no longer he
Who in Alcala took farewell of you
And who presumed in his delicious rapture
To think that he would found the Golden Age
Anew in Spain.—O, that idea was

Childish but divinely beautiful.
Gone are those dreams.—
MARQUIS: Dreams, Prince?—Can they then have
Been nothing more than dreams?
CARLOS: O let me weep,   180
Let me weep scalding tears upon your heart,
My only friend. For I have no one—no one—
In all this great and far-flung earth, no one.
As far out as my father's sceptre reaches,
As far as navigation sends our flags,
There is no place—not one—not one, at which
I may disburden myself of my dreams,
Save here alone. O Roderick, by all
That you and I in times past hoped from Heaven,
Do not expel me from this place, I beg you.   190
MARQUIS (*bends over him in speechless emotion*).
CARLOS: Imagine to yourself I am an orphan
Whom you in pity found beside the throne
And sheltered. I don't know what "father" means—
I am a King's son.—O, if it proves true,
What my heart tells me, if from out of millions
You have been found the one who understands me,
If it is true that forming Nature shaped
A new and second Roderick in Carlos
And in the morning time of our lives set
Our souls' soft harmonies in unison,   200
O, if one tear that can afford me solace
Is dearer to you than my father's favor—
MARQUIS: O dearer than the entire world.
CARLOS: So low
Have I come down—I have become so poor,
That I must call our early childhood years
Back to your mind—that I must beg you to
Discharge those long forgotten debts which you
Incurred while you were still in sailor suits,—
When you and I, two lads wild in our ways,

Were growing up together so like brothers,   210
When no grief weighed on me, except to be
Eclipsed so wholly by your mind,—that I
At last resolved to love you infinitely
Because I lacked the courage to be like you.
Then I began tormenting you with thousands
Of tendernesses and fraternal love.
And you, proud heart, returned them coldly to me.
I often stood—but that you never saw—
With heavy burning teardrops clinging in
My eyes, when you, with disregard for me,   220
Would clasp more humble children in your arms.
Why those? I sadly would exclaim: Do *I*
Not love you too with all my heart?—But you,
You would kneel cold and solemnly before me:
That, as you used to say, beseemed the Prince.

MARQUIS: O silence, Prince, upon those childish stories
Which even now make me flush red with shame.

CARLOS: That I had not deserved from you. My heart
You might disdain and rend, but alienate it,
That you could not. Three times you turned the Prince   230
Away from you, and three times he returned
As suppliant to beg for love from you
And to impose his love on you by force.
A chance then did what Carlos never could.
It happened once amid our playing that
Your shuttlecock flew toward my aunt, the Queen of
Bohemia, and struck her in the eye.
She thought it had been done deliberately
And all in tears brought her complaint straight to
The King. The young folks of the palace had to   240
Appear and name for him the guilty one.
The King vowed to requite most frightfully
That sly insidious trick, though it might be
On his own son.—Just then I saw you standing,
Trembling, at quite some distance off, and then,

Then I stepped forth and threw myself down at
The King's feet. I, I did it, I cried out:
Upon your son fulfill your vengeance.
MARQUIS: Prince,
   What things you force me to recall!
CARLOS: It was:
   In sight of all the courtiers assembled,   250
   Who stood with pity in a circle, it was
   Fulfilled indeed, slave-fashion, on your Charles.
   I looked at you and did not weep. The pain
   Made my teeth lock and clench against each other;
   I did not weep. Beneath the merciless
   Strokes dealt, my royal blood flowed shamefully;
   I looked at you and did not weep.—You came;
   And loudly weeping, fell before my feet.
   Yes, yes, you cried, my pride is overcome.
   I shall repay the debt when you are King.   260
MARQUIS: (gives him his hand.)
   And so I shall, Charles. As a man I now
   Renew that childish pledge. I shall repay.
   Perhaps my hour too will strike.
CARLOS: Now, now—
   O do not waver—it has struck already.
   The time has come when you can make it good.
   I am in need of love.—A monstrous secret
   Is burning in my bosom, and it shall—
   It shall come forth. In your pale countenance
   I seem to read my sentence unto death.
   Listen—freeze—but do not make reply.   270
   I love my mother.
MARQUIS: O my God, my God!
CARLOS: No! I do not want your forbearance. Say it,
   Say that upon this mighty round of earth
   No misery comes close to mine.—Say—But,
   Say what you will, I have already guessed it.
   A son who loves his mother:—world-wide usage,

Nature's order, and the laws of Rome
Condemn that passion. Also, my claim comes
In fearful conflict with my father's rights.
I sense this, yet I go on loving. This way　　　　　　280
Can only lead to madness or the scaffold.
I love with no hope—sacrilegiously—
At peril of my life, in mortal terror—
I see this, yet I go on loving.
MARQUIS:　　　　　　　　　Does
　The Queen know of this passion?
CARLOS:　　　　　　　　　　　How could I
　Reveal myself to her? She is the Queen
　And Philip's wife, and this is Spanish soil.
　Watched by my father's jealousy, hemmed in
　By etiquette on every side, how was
　I to approach her without witnesses?　　　　　290
　Eight hell-tormented months it is now since
　The King recalled me from the upper school
　So that I am condemned to look upon her daily
　And yet remain as silent as the grave.
　Eight hell-tormented months now, Roderick,
　That this fire has been raging in my bosom,
　And that this horrible confession has
　A thousand times kept leaping to my lips
　And yet crept cowardly back to my heart.
　O Roderick—for just a few brief moments　　　300
　Alone with her—
MARQUIS:　　　　　Ah! but your father, Prince—
CARLOS:　Unhappy man! Why must you now remind me
　Of him? Name all the terrors of the conscience,
　But do not name my father to me.
MARQUIS:　You hate your father!
CARLOS:　　　　　　　No! O no! I do
　Not hate my father.—Yet a terror and
　A miscreant's fearfulness come over me
　At the mere mention of that dreaded name.

Can I help if a slavish education
Trod down the tender growth of love when yet   310
My heart was very young?—I had lived only
Six years when for the first time there appeared
Before my eyes that dread man who, as people
Informed me, was my father. It was one morning
When he without the slightest hesitation
Signed four death-warrants. After that I saw
Him only when there was announced to me
My punishment for some misdeed.—My God!
I feel I am becoming bitter—On—
On, on beyond this subject.
MARQUIS: No, you must—   320
   You must disclose your heart now, Prince. By words
   The heavy laden bosom is relieved.
CARLOS: Often I have struggled with myself,
   At midnight often, when my guards were sleeping,
   Thrown myself down with bursts of burning tears
   Before the image of the Blessed Virgin,
   Implored of her a child-like heart,—but always
   Arose with prayer unheard. O Roderick!
   Discover for me this mysterious riddle
   Of Providence:—Why, from a thousand fathers,   330
   Just this one must be mine? Why must he have
   Just this son from a thousand better sons?
   Two opposites more incompatible
   Were never found in all the range of Nature.
   How could she have conjoined these uttermost
   Extremities of all the human race—
   Myself and him—by any bond so sacred?
   O dreadful lot! Why did it have to happen?
   Why did two people who repel each other
   Yet direly have to meet in one desire?   340
   Here, Roderick, you see two hostile stars
   Which in their orbits perpendicular
   One single time in all the course of aeons

14 DON CARLOS

Collide and shatter, then fly off apart
Forever and forever.

MARQUIS: I foresense
A moment of disaster.

CARLOS: So do I.
Horrendous dreams like Furies from the abyss
Pursue me. Dubiously my better mind
Wrestles with my ghastly purposes;
Through labyrinthine sophistries creeps my   350
Unholy subtlety until it stands
Aghast upon the chasm's headlong brink—
O Roderick, if ever I forget
The father in him—Roderick—I see
Your death-pale countenance has caught my meaning—
If ever I forgot the father in him,
What would the King be to me then?

MARQUIS: (*after a silence*)   May I
Presume to ask a favor of my Carlos?
No matter what you plan on doing, will you promise
To undertake no act without your friend?   360
Will you make me this promise?

CARLOS: Anything
Your love enjoins on me. I cast myself
Into your arms entirely.

MARQUIS: It is said
The Monarch plans to come back to the city.
The time is short. If your wish is to see
The Queen in secret, this can take place nowhere
But in Aranjuez. The quiet of
This place—the rural unconstraint or manners
Will favor—

CARLOS: That was what I too had hoped.
But it, alas, was futile!

MARQUIS: Not entirely.   370
I am to go directly to present
Myself to her. If she is still the same

In Spain as once she was at Henry's court,
I shall encounter frankness. If I can
Discover hope for Carlos in her glances,
And find she favors such an interview,—
And if her ladies can be drawn aside—
CARLOS: Most of them are well disposed toward me.
I have won Mondecar especially through
Her son who serves me as a page.
MARQUIS: So much the better.   380
Then you must be close by, Prince, and appear
Immediately when I give you the sign.
CARLOS: I will—I will—But hurry, hurry, now.
MARQUIS: I do not want to lose a single moment.
Farewell, then, Prince, till we meet there.
                (*They leave in different directions.*)

SCENE 2

*The Queen's court in Aranjuez. A simple rural region traversed
by a garden walk and bordered by the Queen's country house.
The Queen. The Duchess of Olivarez. The Princess of Eboli
and the Marquise of Mondecar, who are coming up the garden
walk.*

QUEEN: (*to the Marquise*)
I want to have *you* by me, Mondecar.
The merry eyes of the Princess have been
Tormenting me all morning long. You see,
She scarcely can conceal her pleasure at
Departure from the rural place.
EBOLI: I will not   390
Deny, my Queen, that I look forward with
Delight to being in Madrid again.

MONDECAR: Your Majesty does not feel likewise? Will
  You be so sad to leave Aranjuez?
QUEEN: To leave—this lovely region here at least.
  Here I am, as it were, in my own world.
  I made this place long since my favorite.
  Here I am greeted by my rural Nature,
  That bosom friend of mine from youthful years.   400
  And here I find again my childhood games,
  Here blow the breezes of my native France.
  Do not take this amiss. Our hearts are all
  Drawn to our fatherlands.
EBOLI: But how deserted,
  How dead and dreary it is here! As though
  One were a Trappist.
QUEEN: Quite the opposite.
  I find the deadness only in Madrid.—
  What does our Duchess say to this?
OLIVAREZ: I am,
  Your Majesty, of the opinion that
  It always has been customary to
  Spend one month here, another in the Prado,   410
  And winter in the Residence, as long
  As kings have been in Spain.
QUEEN: Yes, Duchess, as
  You are aware, I always have avoided
  Entering into altercation with you.
MONDECAR: And very soon how lively things will be
  Up in Madrid! The Plaza Mayor will
  Be readied to accommodate a bull fight,
  And we were promised an Auto da Fe
  As well—
QUEEN: Were promised! Do I hear this from
  My gentle Mondecar?
MONDECAR: Why should they not?   420
  What we see in the flames are heretics.
QUEEN: I hope my Eboli thinks otherwise.

EBOLI: I?—O, I beg Your Majesty will not
Consider me a lesser Christian than
The Marquise Mondecar.
QUEEN: O yes, I am
Forgetting where I am.—To other topics.—
Our subject was the country, I believe.
This month has gone by with amazing speed,
It seems. I had expected many joys,
O very many, from this sojourn, and   430
I have not found what I was hoping for.
Do things fare thus with every hope? I can
Not find the wish that disappointed me.
OLIVAREZ: Princess Eboli, you haven't told
Us yet if Gomez is allowed to hope,
Or if we soon shall greet you as his bride.
QUEEN: Yes, Duchess, thank you for reminding me.
                        (*to the Princess*)
I have been asked to intercede with you.
But how can I do that? The man whom I
Reward by giving him my Eboli
Must be a worthy man.   440
OLIVAREZ: Your Majesty,
He is a very worthy man, a man
Whom our most gracious Monarch honors with
His royal favor, as is widely known.
QUEEN: Thereby the man may be made very happy.—
However, we desire to know if he
Can love and can deserve love in return.—
That question, Eboli, I ask of you.
EBOLI: (*stands mute and confused with her eyes cast
      to the ground. Finally she falls at the Queen's feet.*)
Magnanimous Queen, have mercy on me. Let me—
In God's name, let me not become the victim   450
For sacrifice.
QUEEN: For sacrifice? I need
No more. Arise. It is a bitter fate

To be the victim for a sacrifice.
I quite believe you. Rise now.—Is it long
Since you decided to reject the Count?

EBOLI: *(rising)*
O many months. Prince Carlos was still at
The university.

QUEEN: *(is startled and looks at her with searching eyes.)*
                    Have you examined
Yourself to know the reasons for it?

EBOLI: *(with some vehemence)*   Never,
My Queen, this thing can never come about,
Never, for a thousand reasons.

QUEEN: *(very gravely)*   More than one is   460
Too many. You can not esteem him.—That
Is quite enough for me. No more of this.
                    (to the other ladies)
I have not seen the Infanta yet today.
Marquise, bring her to me.

OLIVAREZ: *(looks at the clock.)*   It is not time yet,
Your Majesty.

QUEEN: It is not time yet when
I may be given leave to be a mother?
That is a sorry thing. Do not forget to
Remind me when the time does come.
                    *(A page enters and speaks privately with
                    the chief stewardess, who then turns to the Queen.)*

OLIVAREZ: Marquis
Of Posa, please Your Majesty—

QUEEN: Of Posa?

OLIVAREZ: He comes from France and from the Netherlands 470
And wishes to obtain the favor of
Permission to deliver letters from
Your Regent Mother.

QUEEN: And is this allowed?

OLIVAREZ: *(dubiously)*   Provision
Was not made for this special circumstance

In my instructions, where a Grandee of
Castile comes to deliver letters from
A foreign court and to the Queen of Spain
When she is in her garden arbor.

QUEEN: Then
At my own risk I'll undertake to do so!

OLIVAREZ: Your Majesty, however, will permit   480
Me to withdraw for such time as—

QUEEN: You may
Do as you will on that score, Duchess.

> *(The chief stewardess leaves, and the Queen*
> *beckons toward the page, who immediately withdraws.)*

                          Cavalier,
I bid you welcome here on Spanish soil.

MARQUIS: Which I have never called my fatherland
With such just pride as now—

QUEEN: *(to the two ladies)*   Marquis of Posa,
Who in a knightly tournament at Reims
Once broke a lance in tilting with my father
And three times brought my colors victory,
The first man of his nation to instruct me
How glorious it was to be the Queen   490
Of Spaniards.

> *(turning to the Marquis)*
                          On that last occasion when
We saw each other, Cavalier, up in
The Louvre, you probably would not have dreamed
That you would be my guest here in Castile.

MARQUIS: No, great Queen,—for then I did not dream
That France would lose to us the only thing
That we could possibly still envy her.

QUEEN: Proud Spaniard that you are! The only thing?—
You say this to a daughter of the House of
Valois?

MARQUIS: It is permissible for me   500
To say so now, Your Majesty,—for now

You do belong to us.

QUEEN: I hear your journey
Has taken you through France as well.—What do
You bring me from my most respected mother
And from my much beloved brothers?

MARQUIS: (*hands her the letters.*)
I found your royal mother ill, divorced
From every other joy upon this earth
Except to know her royal daughter happy
Upon the Spanish throne.

QUEEN: How can she fail
To be so with such fond remembrances   510
From loving relatives? or with such sweet
Reminders of—You have seen many courts
And many countries, Cavalier, while on
Your travels, and the ways of many men,—
And now, they say, you have a mind to come
Yourself and settle in your native land?
A greater prince within your quiet walls than
King Philip on his throne—as a free man!
As a philosopher!—I greatly doubt
You will be pleased with living in Madrid.   520
One is so—quiet in Madrid.

MARQUIS: And that
Is more than all the rest of Europe has
To be contented over.

QUEEN: So I hear.
I have unlearned this world's concerns, almost
To where I have unlearned the memory of them.
                (*to the Princess of Eboli*)
Princess Eboli, I think I see
A hyacinth in bloom up there.—Would you
Go fetch it for me?
        (*The Princess goes toward the place. The Queen
        speaks in a somewhat softer voice to the Marquis.*)
                Cavalier, I should

Be much deceived if your arrival had not
Made one more person happy at this court.   530
MARQUIS: I found a man weighed down with sadness, whom
  Only a certain something in this world
  Could gladden—
       (*The Princess returns with the flower.*)
EBOLI: Since the Cavalier has seen
  So many countries, he will doubtless have
  A fund of things of note to tell us of.
MARQUIS: You may be sure of that. Everyone knows
  That seeking of adventure is the duty
  Of knights,—and that the sacredest of all
  Is to protect all ladies.
MONDECAR: Yes, from giants.
  But now there are no giants any more.   540
MARQUIS: Force always is a giant to the weak.
QUEEN: The Cavalier is right. There still are giants,
  But no more knights.
MARQUIS: Quite recently, upon
  My journey back from Naples, I was witness
  To a most touching story which the holy
  Legacy of friendship made my own.—
  If I were not compelled to fear that I
  Might weary you, Your Majesty, with my
  Account of it—
QUEEN: Do I have any choice?
  The Princess' curiosity will not   550
  Permit the slightest thing to be withheld.
  Proceed. I am myself a friend of stories.
MARQUIS: Two noble houses in Mirandola,
  Tired of their jealousy and ancient feuding
  Which from the Ghibellines and Guelfs had been
  Their legacy for centuries, decided
  To join by means of tender bonds of marriage
  Together in an everlasting peace.
  The nephew of the powerful Pietro,

Fernando, and the beautiful Mathilde,   560
Colonna's daughter, were selected to
Conjoin this lovely bond of unity.
Two nobler hearts were never formed by Nature
For one another,—never had the world
Judged any choice more fortunate than this.
Till then Fernando had adored his bride
Solely through the medium of her portrait.—
But how Fernando trembled when he found
What his most ardent expectations had
Not ventured to believe from that mere picture!   570
In Padua where studies still detained him
Fernando waited only for the moment
Which would grant him the opportunity
To throw himself before Mathilde's feet
And stammer the first homage of his love.

> (*The Queen becomes more attentive. After a brief silence
> the Marquis continues the narrative, directing it, inso-
> far as the Queen's presence permits, rather to the
> Princess of Eboli.*)

Meanwhile by virtue of his spouse's death
Pietro's hand is freed.—With youthful ardor
The aging man devours the voice of rumor
Which was effusive in Mathilde's praise.
He comes! He sees!—He loves! His new emotion   580
Drowns out the gentler voice of Nature now.
The uncle woos his nephew's promised bride
And consecrates his theft before the altar.

QUEEN: What does Fernando then decide?
MARQUIS: On wings of love,
And of the frightful change quite unaware,
Joy-frenzied he posts to Mirandola.
By starlight his swift steed arrives before
The gates.—A din as though of Bacchanals
At dances and at drums comes thundering
Toward him from the illuminated palace.   590

He staggers up the stair and sees himself
Unrecognized in that loud festive hall, where
Amid the reeling revel of his guests
Pietro sat,—an angel at his side,
An angel whom Fernando knows, who even
In dreams had not appeared so radiant.
A single glance shows him what he had once
Possessed, shows him what he has lost forever.

EBOLI: Unfortunate Fernando!

QUEEN: Cavalier,
  Your tale is over, is it not?—It must   600
  Be over.

MARQUIS: Not entirely.

QUEEN: Did you not
  Say also that Fernando was your friend?

MARQUIS: I have none dearer.

EBOLI: But continue with
  Your story, Cavalier.

MARQUIS: It now becomes
  Quite melancholy,—and the recollection
  Renews my grief. Permit me to dispense
  With the conclusion—

                    (*general silence*)

QUEEN: (*turns to the Princess of Eboli.*)
                    Now they surely will
  At last allow me to embrace my daughter.—
  Princess, bring her to me.

  (*The latter withdraws. The Marquis beckons to a page,
  who appears at the rear and disappears again immediately. The Queen opens the letters which the Marquis
  has given her and seems to be surprised. During this time
  the Marquis speaks privately and very urgently with the
  Marquise of Mondecar.—The Queen has read the letters
  and turns toward the Marquis with a searching glance.*)
                    But you have   610
Said nothing of Mathilde? Possibly

She does not know how much Fernando suffers?
MARQUIS: Mathilde's heart no one has fathomed yet,—
    But noble souls endure in silence.
QUEEN: You glance about? Whom are you searching for?
MARQUIS: I was just thinking of how glad a certain
    Person, whom I dare not name, would be
    In my place.
QUEEN: Whose fault is it that he is
    Not here?
MARQUIS: *(quickly taking her up)*
         What? May I be so bold
    As to interpret that as I would like?—
    He would find pardon if he came here now?   620
QUEEN: *(frightened)*
    Right now, Marquis? What do you mean by that?
MARQUIS: He really might dare hope—might he?
QUEEN: *(with increasing confusion)*   You frighten me,
    Marquis,—He surely would not—
MARQUIS: Here he is.
        (Enter Carlos. The Marquis of Posa and the
         Marquise of Mondecar retire toward the rear.)
CARLOS: *(on his knees before the Queen)*
    Ah, so the moment has arrived at last,
    And Charles may touch this dear hand finally!
QUEEN: What a thing to do!—and what a mad
    And culpable surprise! Get up! We may
    Be taken unawares. My court is near.
CARLOS: I will not rise—here I shall kneel forever.
    On this spot I shall lie in fast enchantment   630
    And rooted fixedly in this position—
QUEEN: Madman!
    To what audacity are you led by
    My favor? Do you realize that this
    Presumptuous language is directed to
    Your Queen, your mother? Do you realize
    That I—that I myself might tell the King

Of this invasion—

CARLOS: And that I must die!
　Let them hale me to the scaffold straight
　From here. One moment spent in Paradise
　Will not be bought too dearly with my death.   640

QUEEN: And yet your Queen?

CARLOS: O Heaven! I will go—
　I will leave you.—Am I not forced to do so
　If you demand it *this* way? Mother! Mother!
　How horribly you toy with me! A gesture,
　A sound from your lips, or a mere half-glance
　Commands me to exist or pass away.
　What further wish is yours that shall be done?
　What can there be yet underneath the sun
　That I will not make haste to sacrifice
　If you desire it?

QUEEN: Flee!

CARLOS: O God in heaven!   650

QUEEN: The only thing, Charles, that I beg of you
　With tears is—Flee!—before my ladies come—
　Before my jailers find the two of us
　Together here and to your father's ears
　Report the dreadful tidings—

CARLOS: I await my fate—
　No matter if it be for life or death.
　What? Have I concentrated all my hopes
　Upon this single moment which now gives
　You to me finally in privacy
　Just so false fears might disappoint me at   660
　The goal? No, Queen! The world may wheel about
　Its pole a hundred or a thousand times
　Before chance brings this favor once again.

QUEEN: Nor shall it do so through eternity.
　Unhappy man! What do you want of me?

CARLOS: O Queen, God is my witness I have struggled,
　Have struggled as no mortal man before

Has ever struggled—Queen!—to no avail!
My hero's strength has left me. I succumb.

QUEEN: No more of this!—Respect my peace of mind.   670

CARLOS: You once were mine—in the eyes of the world
Two great thrones had affianced you to me,
And God and Nature had adjudged you mine,
But Philip, Philip, he has robbed me of you—

QUEEN: He is your father.

CARLOS: And your husband.

QUEEN: Who
Bequeaths to you the world's most mighty kingdom.

CARLOS: And *you* as mother—

QUEEN: You are raving wildly—

CARLOS: And does he know how rich he is? Has he
A heart of feeling that can value yours?
No, I do not want to complain, I want to   680
Forget how happy beyond words to tell *I* would
Have been to have your hand—if only *he* were.
But he is not.—That is the hellish torment!
He is not and he never will be so.
Fate took away my heaven only to
Exterminate it in King Philip's arms.

QUEEN: Atrocious thought!

CARLOS: O I am quite aware
Who was the founder of this marriage,—I
Know Philip's way of loving and of wooing.
Who are you in this kingdom? Let me tell you.   690
The Regent? Not a bit of it! If *you*
Were Regent, could these Albas massacre?
Could Flanders go on bleeding for the Faith?
Or are you Philip's wife? Impossible!
That I can not believe. A wife possesses
Her husband's heart.—To whom does his belong?
For every tenderness that may escape him
In ardor, does he not apologize
To his grey hair as well as to his sceptre?

QUEEN: Who told you that my lot at Philip's side   700
  Was pitiable?
CARLOS: My heart, which fiercely feels
  How enviable it would have been at *my* side,
  Has told me so.
QUEEN: O man of vanity!
  What if *my* heart told me the opposite?
  And what if the respectful tenderness
  Of Philip, and the mute speech of his love,
  Had far more intimate appeal for me
  Than his proud son's audacious eloquence?
  If an old man's maturely weighed respect—
CARLOS: That is another matter.—Then—forgive me.   710
  I did not realize you loved the King.
QUEEN: To honor him is my desire and pleasure.
CARLOS: Then you have never loved?
QUEEN: A curious question!
CARLOS: Then you have never loved?
QUEEN: —I love no longer.
CARLOS: Because your heart, because your vows forbid it?
QUEEN: Prince, leave me now, and never come again
  For any such an interview as this.
CARLOS: Because your vows, because your heart forbids it?
QUEEN: Because my obligation—Wretched man,
  Why drearily anatomize the fate   720
  Which you and I must still obey?
CARLOS: We must?
  We must obey?
QUEEN: What do you mean by this
  Tone of solemnity?
CARLOS: Precisely this:
  That Carlos is not minded to be forced
  When he may do his will; that Carlos is
  Not minded to remain the wretchedest
  Of men in this realm when it costs no more
  Than the subversion of the laws to be

The happiest.

QUEEN: Can I have understood you?
You still have hopes? You still presume to hope   730
When everything already has been lost?

CARLOS: I reckon nothing lost except the dead.

QUEEN: You still have hopes of me, hopes of your mother?—
           (*She looks at him long and penetratingly,—*
                      then with dignity and gravity.)
Why not? As newly chosen King you can
Do more than that.—You can destroy by fire
The ordinances of the departed King,
Can overthrow his statues, you can even—
Who will prevent it?—from its resting place
In the Escurial drag forth the dead
Man's mummy to the light of day and strew   740
His desecrated dust to the four winds,
And finally, to finish properly,—

CARLOS: In Heaven's name, do not complete the list.

QUEEN: And finally can marry with your mother.

CARLOS: Accursed son!
           (*He stands a moment motionless and speechless.*)
                      Yes, it is over now.
All over.—Bright and clear I feel what was
Meant to remain forever dark to me.
For me you are a thing gone by—gone by—
Gone by—forever.—Now the die is cast.
You are lost wholly to me.—O, in this   750
I feel my hell! Another hell lies in
Possessing you.—Alas! I cannot grasp it,
My nerves are stretched now to the snapping point.

QUEEN: Dear Charles, fit subject for my tears! I feel—
I wholly feel the nameless suffering
Now raging in your bosom. Boundless is
Your sorrow, like your love. But boundless also
Is the renown of conquest over it.
Achieve that, youthful hero, for the prize

Is worthy of this strong and lofty fighter,   760
And worthy of the youth through whose heart rolls
The virtue of so many royal forebears.
Take courage, noble Prince.—The grandson of
Great Charles begins to wrestle with fresh strength
Where sons of other men leave off despondent.

CARLOS: Too late! My God, it is too late!

QUEEN: To be
A man? O Charles, how great becomes our virtue
When our hearts break by dint of practice of it!
You were high placed by Providence,—much higher,
Prince, than were millions of your other brethren.   770
With partiality she gave her favorite
What she from others took away, and millions
Ask whether he, by virtue of his birth,
Deserved to be more than we other mortals.
Up! Justify what Heaven has thus sanctioned!
Deserve to walk first in the world's procession,
Surrender what no other has surrendered.

CARLOS: That I can do.—To fight for you and win you,
I have a giant's strength; to lose you, none.

QUEEN: Acknowledge, Carlos, that it is defiance   780
And bitterness and pride which now draw your
Desires so madly toward your mother. That
Same love, that heart, which you would waste on me
Belongs to those realms over which one day
You are to rule. You see, you dissipate
The substance trusted to you by your ward.
Love is your noble office. Until now
It has strayed to your mother.—Bring it back,
O bring it to your future kingdoms, and,
Instead of daggers of the conscience, feel   790
The joy of being God. Elizabeth
Was your first love. Now let your second love
Be Spain. How gladly, my good Charles, will I
Yield place before the loftier Beloved.

CARLOS: *(overcome with emotion, throws himself at her feet.)*
How grand you are, Divine One!—Everything
You ask, I shall perform!—So be it then!
                         (He rises.)
I stand here now in the Almighty's hand
And swear to you, swear everlasting—No!
O Heaven! only everlasting silence,
But never to forget.
QUEEN: How could I ever   800
Require from Carlos what I am myself
Unwilling to perform?
MARQUIS: *(rushing up the garden walk)*
                         The King!
QUEEN: O Heaven!
MARQUIS: Away from here, Prince, quickly!
QUEEN: His suspicion
Will be appalling if he sees you—
CARLOS: I
Shall stay!
QUEEN: And who will be the victim then?
CARLOS: *(takes the Marquis by the arm.)*
Come, Roderick!
             (He leaves and comes back again.)
                 What may I take with me?
QUEEN: The friendship of your mother.
CARLOS: Friendship! Mother!
QUEEN: And also these tears from the Netherlands.
   *(She gives him several letters. Charles and the Marquis
   leave. The Queen glances about uneasily for her ladies,
   who are nowhere to be seen. As she starts to walk back
   toward the rear, the King appears.*
   *Enter the King, the Duke of Alba, Count Lerma, Domingo;
   also various ladies and grandees who remain some dis-
   tance off.)*
KING: *(looks about with surprise and is silent for a time.)*
What do I see! You here! Alone, Madame!

And not a single lady in attendance?   810
I am amazed.—Where are your waiting-women?
QUEEN: Most gracious spouse—
KING: Why are you here alone?
                    (to his retinue)
For this unpardonable oversight
The strictest reckoning is due to me.
Whose was the charge of waiting on the Queen?
Whose turn was it to serve her here today?
QUEEN: Do not be angry, o my spouse,—I am
Myself the guilty one.—At my command
The Princess Eboli withdrew from here.
KING: At your command?
QUEEN: To fetch the nursemaid in,   820
Because I had so longed for the Infanta.
KING: And therefore you dismissed all your attendants?
But this excuses only the first lady.
Where was the second one?
MONDECAR:

(who meanwhile has returned and mingled with the other
    ladies, steps forward.)
                              Your Majesty,
I feel that I am guilty—
KING: For that reason
I hereby grant you ten years' time far from
Madrid in which to meditate upon it.
    (The Marquise steps back with tears in her eyes. General
    silence. Everyone looks in dismay at the Queen.)
QUEEN: Marquise, whom are you weeping for?
                    (to the King)   If I
Have erred, most gracious spouse, the royal crown
Of this great kingdom, toward which I myself   830
Have never stretched my hand, should have at least
Protected me from any cause to blush.
Is there a law within this realm that summons
Monarchs' daughters to the bar of justice?

Does force alone guard women here in Spain?
Does any witness but their virtue shield them?
And now, my spouse, forgive me,—I am not
Accustomed to dismiss in tears those who
With joy have done my service.—Mondecar!
>   *(She takes off her chain-belt and hands it*
>   *to the Marquise.)*
The King is angered with you,—I am not—   840
Therefore accept this token of my favor
And of this hour.—Avoid this realm henceforth.—
You have offended nowhere but in Spain;
At home in France such tears are wiped away
With joys.—O must I always be reminded!
>   *(She leans upon the chief stewardess*
>   *and covers her face.)*
In my France it was otherwise.

KING: *(in some confusion)*   Can you
Have been upset by a reproach born of
My love? Or by a word which was laid on
My lips by most affectionate concern?
>   *(He turns to the grandezza.)*
Here stand the vassals of my throne assembled.   850
Did ever sleep descend upon my eyelids
Without my having reckoned on the evening
Of each day how my nations' hearts were beating
Throughout my furthest-flung meridians?—
And should I be more anxiously concerned
For my throne's sake than for my own heart's spouse?—
My nations can be vouched for by my sword,
And by—the Duke of Alba: but this eye
Alone can vouch for my wife's love.

QUEEN: If I
Have given you offense, my husband—

KING: I   860
Am called the richest man in Christendom;
Upon my empire the sun never sets—

But that another has possessed before me
And after me still others will possess.
But *this* is mine. What is the King's, belongs
To Fortune—but Elizabeth belongs
To Philip. Here's the spot where I am mortal.

QUEEN: You are afraid, Sire?

KING: Surely not of this
Grey hair? Once I begin to be afraid,
I have already ceased to be afraid.—   870
                    (*to the grandees*)
I count the grandees of my court.—The main
One is not here. Where is Don Carlos, my
Infante?
                    (*No one answers.*)
                    This youth Charles begins to fill me
With apprehension. Since returning from
School in Alcala he avoids my presence.
His blood is hot, why is his glance so cold?
So calculatedly reserved his bearing?
Be vigilant, I recommend.

ALBA: I shall be.
As long as my heart beats against this armor
Don Philip may with safety go to sleep.   880
Duke Alba stands before the throne like God's
Own cherub by the gate of Paradise.

LERMA: May I presume in all humility
To contradict the wisest of all kings?—
I honor my King's Majesty too much
To judge his son so fast and so severely.
I do fear much from Carlos' fiery blood,
But nothing from his heart.

KING: Lord Count of Lerma,
You speak effectively to soothe the father:
The King's support will be the Duke, however—   890
No more of this—
                    (*He turns toward his retinue.*)

I haste now to Madrid.
My royal office summons me. The pest
Of heresy infects my peoples and
Disorder rises in my Netherlands.
It is high time. A terrible example
Shall bring back those in error to the truth.
The great oath that all kings in Christendom
Have sworn I shall myself redeem tomorrow.
This execution shall outdo all custom;
My entire court is solemnly invited.   900

> (*He conducts the Queen away.*
> *The others follow.*)

SCENE 3

*Don Carlos, with letters in his hand, and the Marquis of Posa,
enter from opposite sides.*

CARLOS: I have decided. Flanders shall be saved.
   She wishes it.— That is enough for me.
MARQUIS: No further moment must be lost. The Duke
   Of Alba was appointed in the council
   As governor, they say.
CARLOS: First thing tomorrow
   I shall ask for an audience with my father.
   I shall demand this office for myself.
   It is the first request I ever dared
   To make of him. He cannot well refuse me.
   He long has disapproved my being in   910
   Madrid. And what a welcome pretext to
   Get me away. And Roderick,— shall I
   Confess— I further hope— perhaps I shall
   When face to face with him be able to
   Restore myself again to his good favor.
   He never yet has heard the voice of Nature.

Let me experiment then, Roderick,
And see what it can do upon my lips!
MARQUIS: At last I hear once more my Carlos speaking!
You are yourself again at last.
               (*Enter Count Lerma.*)
LERMA: The Monarch   920
Has just departed from Aranjuez.
I have the order—
CARLOS: Very well, Count Lerma.
I shall arrive there with the King.
MARQUIS: (*makes as though to withdraw. With some formality.*)
                 Your Highness
Has nothing further with which you would charge me?
CARLOS: Nothing, Cavalier. I wish you luck
On your arrival in Madrid. You shall
Recount still further things concerning Flanders.
        (*to Lerma, who is still waiting*)
I'll come with you at once.
            (*Exit Lerma.*)
                I understand you.
I thank you. Only a third party's presence,
However, will excuse this cold restraint.   930
Are we not brothers?— Let this farce of rank
Be banished in the future from our union.
Imagine that the two of us had met
Each other masked and costumed at a ball,
You in a slave's attire, and I, from whim,
Disguised in royal purple. As long as
The carnival goes on let us respect
The lie, play out our roles in jesting earnest,
And not undo the mob's sweet dream-illusion.
Through his disguise your Charles will beckon to you,   940
And you as you pass by will press my hand,
And we shall understand.
MARQUIS: The dream is godlike.
But will it not fly off and vanish? Is

My Charles so very certain of resisting
The lures of majesty unlimited?
There is a great day yet to come— a day
When this heroic spirit will— I warn you—
Fail in a test severe. Don Philip dies.
And Charles inherits the most mighty realm
In Christendom.— A monstrous gap will then   950
Remove him from the race of mortal men,
And he who yesterday was still a man,
Today is God. He has no weaknesses.
His duties toward eternity grow mute.
Humanity— a great word in his ear
Today— sells out and crawls among its idols.
Compassion dies in him when sorrows die,
His virtue dulls amid voluptuousnesses,
Peru sends gold for payment of his follies,
His court spawns devils for his vices. Drowsing,   960
He falls to drunken sleep amid this heaven
Which slaves have cunningly built up around him.
His godhood lasts the same length as his dream.—
Woe to the madman who from pity wakes him.
But what would then become of Roderick?—
Friendship is true and bold— weak majesty
Will not endure its awful ray. You would
Not tolerate the citizen's defiance,
Nor I the Prince's pride.

CARLOS: Your picturing
Of monarchs is both true and terrible.   970
Yes, I believe you.— But voluptuousness
Alone unlocked their hearts to vice.— I am
Still chaste, a youth of twenty-three. What thousands
Before me squandered conscienceless amid
Embraces of debauchery,— that is
The best half of their spirits, manly strength,
I have kept stored up for the future ruler.
What possibly could drive you from my heart

If women cannot?
MARQUIS: I myself. Could I
  Love you so fervently, Charles, if I were   980
  Obliged to fear you?
CARLOS: That will never happen.
  Do you have need of me? Do you have passions
  That grovel at the throne? Does gold entice you?
  You are a richer subject far than I
  As King shall ever be.— Are you possessed
  By greed for honor? As a youth you had
  Consumed its measure—you rejected it.
  Which one will be the other's creditor,
  And which the other's debtor?—You are silent?
  You shrink before temptation? Are you so
  Uncertain of yourself?   990
MARQUIS: I yield.
  Here is my hand.
CARLOS: You're mine?
MARQUIS: Eternally,
  And to the furthest scope of that word's meaning.
CARLOS: Pledged just as true and warm hereafter to
  The King as now today to the Infante?
MARQUIS: I swear it.
CARLOS: Even when the dragon of
  Hypocrisy holds my unguarded heart
  Within its grip— when these eyes have unlearned
  The tears that once they wept— these ears are bolted
  And barred to supplication,— will you then,   1000
  As the intrepid guardian of my virtue,
  Take hold of me with strength and summon up
  My Genius by its great name?
MARQUIS: I will.
CARLOS: And now one further favor. Call me Carlos.[1]
  I always envied those of you who had
  That right of intimacy. That brotherly
  First name beguiles my ear, my heart, with sweetest

Intimations of equality.
No objection—I can guess your thought. To you
I know it is a trifle—but so much   1010
To me, the King's son. Will you be my brother?
MARQUIS: Your brother, Carlos!
CARLOS: To the King now. No
More fears beset me.—Arm in arm with you,
I dare my century to do me battle.   (1014)

(*Exeunt.*)

---

[1] It has been necessary in translation to adapt slightly lines 1004-1012. What Don Carlos asks of Marquis Posa is to be addressed as "Du," i.e. with the intimate "thou-form" of the verb. Since this verb form is archaic in English, its nearest equivalent, the use of the first name, has been selected even though this is not wholly consistent with the foregoing text. Posa's change of tone is indicated in German (line 1012) by the words "*Dein* Bruder" (without the name "Carlos") instead of "*Ihr* Bruder." Throughout the remainder of the play Posa will address Carlos as "thou."

ACT II

In the royal palace in Madrid.
King Philip beneath the throne-canopy. At some distance from
the King, the Duke of Alba, with covered head. Carlos.

CARLOS: The kingdom takes precedence. Carlos will
  Most gladly stand down for the Minister.
  He speaks for Spain—I am the family son.
  (He steps back with a bow.)
PHILIP: The Duke shall stay, and the Infánt may speak.
CARLOS: *(turning to Alba)*
  Then from *your* generosity, Lord Duke,
  I must entreat the King by way of gift.   1020
  A child— you realize— may have upon
  His heart extensive matters for his father
  Ill suiting a third party's ear. The King
  Shall not be taken from you,— I wish only
  To have my father during this brief hour.
PHILIP: Here stands his friend.
CARLOS: But have I won the right
  To claim that I have found the like in him?
PHILIP: Or ever sought to win?—I do not like
  These sons who hit on better choices than
  Their fathers.
CARLOS: Can the Duke of Alba's knightly   1030
  Pride endure to listen to this scene?
  For as I live, I would not want, by God—
  Not even if it cost a diadem—
  To play the rash impertinent who does

39

Not blush to force his way unasked between
A father and his son and damns himself
To stand there crushed by the awareness of
His insignificance.

PHILIP: (*gets up, casting an angry glance at the Prince.*)
                    Withdraw Lord Duke.
    (*The latter goes toward the main door,
       through which Carlos had come; the King
       beckons him toward a different one.*)
No, to my study, till I call you.

CARLOS: (*as soon as the Duke has left the room, goes up
      to the King and kneels before him in the
      expression of the greatest emotion.*)
                                        Now
My father once again, mine once again—
I thank you for this favor— Father, give me   1040
Your hand— O blessed day— The rapture of
This kiss went long ungranted to your child.
Why have you banished me so long, my Father,
Out of your heart? What is it I have done?

PHILIP: Infánt, your heart knows nothing of these wiles.
Save them, I do not like them.

CARLOS: (*rising*)   That was it!
Ah, there I hear your courtiers.—My Father!
It is not good, by God! not everything,
Not everything a priest says, nor not all   1050
The things said by the toadies of a priest.
I am not evil, Father— hot blood is
My wickedness— My only crime is youth.
I am not wicked, really wicked,—even
If savage seethings do accuse my heart
Sometimes. My heart is good.

PHILIP: Your heart is pure,
I know that, like your prayers.

CARLOS: It must be now or never!
We are alone. The fearful barrier

Of etiquette between a son and father
Has fallen. Now or never! A ray of hope   1060
Begins to gleam in me, and through my heart
Flies a sweet premonition.— All of Heaven
Stoops down with troops of angels, and
With full emotion the Thrice-Holy gazes
Upon the great and lovely scene.— My Father!
Atonement!

                    (He falls at his feet.)

PHILIP: Let me go! Get up!
CARLOS: Atonement!
PHILIP: *(tries to pull away from him.)*
  This farce is getting out of hand for me—
CARLOS: Your own child's love is out of hand?
PHILIP: Tears, yet?
  Disgraceful spectacle!—Go, leave my sight.
CARLOS: Atonement, Father— now or never!
PHILIP: Out,   1070
  Out of my sight! Come loaded with disgrace
Home from my battles and my arms will be
Wide open to receive you.—As you are,
I disavow you.— Only coward's guilt
Will infamously grow from outbursts such
As this. He who repents without a blush
Will never stint repentance.
CARLOS: Who is that?
  By what misunderstanding has this alien
Strayed in among mankind?— Why, tears are always
The attestation to humanity.   1080
His eyes are dry, no woman gave him birth—
O, force those never moistened eyes of yours
To learn tears while there still is time, or else—
Or else you may yet have to make up for it
In a hard hour to come.
PHILIP: Do you imagine you will shake your father's
  Serious doubts with pretty speeches?

CARLOS: Doubts?
   I mean to wipe it out, this doubt.—I mean
   To hang upon my father's heart, and pull,
   Pull furiously upon this father's heart   1090
   Until the stony sheath of doubt upon
   This heart is shed away.—Who are these people
   Who drive me from the favor of my King?
   How much has the monk bid the father for
   His son? And what will Alba offer him
   To compensate a childless, squandered life?
   Do you want love?—Then here within this bosom
   There springs a fountain fresher, fierier
   Than in the muddy, swampy cisterns which
   Must first be tapped with Philip's gold.
PHILIP: Stop there,   1100
   Presumptuous fool!—The men you dare to slander
   Are tried and proven servants of my choosing
   And you will yet revere them.
CARLOS: Never. Never.
   I know my value. What your Albas do,
   Charles can do also, and Charles can do more.
   What does a hireling care about a kingdom
   That never will be his—Or what is *his*
   Concern if Philip's grey hair turns to white?
   Your Carlos would have loved you.—I am filled
   With horror at the thought of being all   1110
   Alone and lonely on a *throne.*—
PHILIP: (*struck by these words, stands pensive and
    brooding. After a pause*)
                  I *am* alone.
CARLOS: (*going up to him with eagerness and warmth*)
   You were. O do not hate me any more,
   I'll love you filially and ardently,
   But do not hate me any more.—How sweet,
   How wonderful it is to feel ourselves

Exalted in a noble soul, to know
Our joy brings color to the cheeks of others,
Our anguish trembles in another heart,
Our suffering brings tears to other eyes—
How glorious it is, and fine, to hasten   1120
Hand in hand with a beloved son
Back down the rosy path of youth and once
Again to dream the dream of life,—how great,
How lovely to endure in one's child's virtue
Immortal and unperishing, conferring
Beneficence for centuries!—How fine
To sow what a dear son will one day harvest,
To gather what will bring him gain, to guess
How high his gratitude will flame!—My Father,
About this earthly Paradise your monks
Are very wisely silent.   1130

PHILIP: (*not without emotion*) O my son,
My son! You break the staff above yourself.
You paint joys which—you never granted me.

CARLOS: Of that, may God Omniscient be the judge!—
You, *you* excluded me yourself from any
Share of sceptre or of father's heart.
Until today—O was that good, or fair?—
Till now, I, Spain's hereditary Prince,
Was forced to be an alien here in Spain,
A captive on this soil where I some day   1140
Shall be the ruler. Was that just, or kind?—
How often, O how often, Father, have I
Looked down for shame when emissaries from
The potentates abroad, when news accounts
Told me the latest of the court here in
Aranjuez.

PHILIP: Blood rages in your veins
Too wildly, you would only ruin things.

CARLOS: Assign me things to ruin, Father,—wildly

My pulses rage—I am age twenty-three,
And nothing done for immortality!   1150
I am aroused, I feel my worth.—I hear
The knocking of my summons to the throne
Wake me, like a believer, from my slumber,
And all lost hours of my youth exhort
Me loud as debts of honor. It has come,
That grand and noble moment which at last
Requires of me the great pound's interest:
World history, ancestral glory, summon
Me, and the thundrous trumpet of Renown.
The time has now arrived to open for me   1160
The glorious tournament of Fame.—My King,
May I now dare to utter the request
That brings me here?

PHILIP: Still a request in store?
Declare it.

CARLOS: The rebellion in Brabant
Swells threateningly. The rebels' stubbornness
Demands a skillful, strong defense. To tame
The hotheads' fury now the Duke is being
Despatched to lead an army into Flanders
Equipped with sovereign powers from the King.
How honorable this office is, and how   1170
Entirely suitable to introduce
Your son into the temple of Renown!—
To me, my King, to me entrust this army.
The Netherlanders love me; I shall venture
To pledge my blood to prove their loyalty.

PHILIP: You talk like one within a dream. This office
Requires a man and not a boy—

CARLOS: Requires
A human being, Father, and that is
The one thing that Duke Alba never has been.

PHILIP: And terror can alone subdue revolt,   1180

Compassion would be madness.—No, my son,
Your heart is soft, the Duke is held in awe—
Desist from your request.

CARLOS: Send me along
Then with the army into Flanders, risk
That much on my soft heart. The mere name of
The royal Prince which will fly on before
My banners will make conquests where the Duke
Of Alba's hangmen work mere devastation.
I make this supplication on my knees.
It is the first request in all my life—   1190
Trust Flanders, Father, to my hands—

PHILIP: (*looking at the Infante with a piercing gaze*)
                         And with
It, my best army to your lust for power?
The dagger to my murderer?

CARLOS: My God!
Am I no further on? Is such the fruit
Of this great hour solicited so long?
     (*after some reflection, with mitigated earnestness*)
Give me a gentler answer. Do not send
Me *thus* away. I should not like to be
Dismissed with this aggrieving answer, nor
To be dismissed with such a heavy heart.
Deal with me more benevolently. It is   1200
My urgent need, my final desperate
Attempt—I cannot understand, I cannot
Endure steadfastly like a man, that you
Refuse me everything and everything
And everything this way. Let me withdraw now.
Unheard I leave your presence, disappointed
In a thousand sweet anticipations.
Your Albas and Domingos will in triumph
Throne where your child today wept in the dust.
The throng of courtiers, the timorous   1210

Grandees, the death-pale league of monks were witness
When you accorded me this formal hearing.
Do not put me to shame! O do not, Father,
Wound me so mortally as to abandon
Me to the court's derisive insolence
That strangers gorge upon your favor while
Your Carlos can get nothing that he asks.
To show you mean to honor me, send me
To Flanders with the army.

PHILIP: Do not speak
Those words again, on pain of your King's anger!   1220
CARLOS: I brave the anger of my King and ask
A final time—Trust Flanders to my hands.
I must and shall leave Spain. My living here
Is fetching breath beneath the hangman's hand.—
Heavy lies the sky upon me in
Madrid, like the awareness of a murder.
Swift change of sky alone can make me well.
If you have any wish to save me, send me
Without delay to Flanders.

PHILIP: (*with forced calmness*)   Sick men such
As you, my son, have need of nursing care   1230
And dwell beneath physicians' eyes. You will
Remain in Spain; the Duke will go to Flanders.

CARLOS: (*beside himself*)
O stand about me now, good spirits—

PHILIP: (*retreating a step*)   Stop!
What is the meaning of these gestures?

CARLOS: (*with faltering voice*)   Father,
Is this decision quite irrevocable?

PHILIP: It issued from the King.

CARLOS: My task is done.

(*He leaves in vehement agitation.*)

(*Philip remains standing for a time plunged in sombre reflection. Finally he walks several paces up and down the
room. Alba approaches with embarrassment.*)

PHILIP: Stand ready for the order any hour
  To leave for Brussels.
ALBA: Everything is ready,
  My King.
PHILIP: Your authorization for full powers
  Lies sealed already in my study. Meanwhile   1240
  Take your departure from the Queen, and as
  You leave, present yourself to the Infante.
ALBA: With gestures such as raving madmen make
  I saw him walk out of this room just now.
  Your royal Majesty is also quite
  Perturbed and seems to be profoundly shaken—
  Perhaps the subject of the conversation—?
PHILIP: (after some pacing back and forth)
  The subject was Duke Alba.
                (The King stops with his eye fixed
                      upon him. Sombrely)
                             I may like
  To hear that Carlos hates my ministers;
  But with annoyance I discover he   1250
  Despises them.
              (Alba turns pale and starts to protest.)
                    No answer for the present.
  I give you leave to make peace with the Prince.
ALBA: Sire!
PHILIP: Tell me who it was that warned me in
  The first place of my son's black-hued designs?
  I listened then to you but not to him.
  I'll put this to the test, Duke. Carlos shall
  Henceforth stand closer to my throne. Now go.
                (The King withdraws to his study.
                The Duke goes away by a different door.)

SCENE 2

An anteroom to the Queen's apartments.
Enter Don Carlos through the middle door in conversation
with a page. At his coming the courtiers who are in the ante-
room disperse in the adjoining rooms.

CARLOS: A note to me?—Then what is this key for?
   And both delivered in such secrecy?
   Come closer.—Where did you come by this?
PAGE: *(mysteriously)*   As   1260
   The Lady strictly told me, she would rather
   Be guessed than be described—
CARLOS: *(stepping back)*   You say "the Lady"?
                (scrutinizing the page more closely)
   What?—How?—Who are you then?
ALBA: I am a page
   In service to her Majesty the Queen—
   (in fright advancing on him and putting his hand over his
   mouth)
CARLOS: Quiet, or you will die! I know enough.
   (He hastily breaks the seal and steps to the furthest corner of
   the room to read the letter. Meanwhile the Duke of Alba
   enters and, without being noticed by the Prince, passes
   him on his way into the Queen's apartments. Carlos be-
   gins to tremble violently and alternately to flush and
   turn pale. After he has finished reading he stands for a
   long time speechless with his eyes fixed and staring at
   the letter.—Finally he turns to the page.)
   She gave you this herself?
PAGE: With her own hands.
CARLOS: She gave you this herself?—O do not mock me!
   I have not yet read anything she wrote,
   I am obliged to trust you if you swear it.
   But if it was a lie, confess it frankly   1270

And do not make a fool of me.

PAGE: Of whom?

CARLOS:

(glances at the letter again and looks at the page with dubious, probing gaze. After he has made a turn through the
room)

Your parents are alive? Your father serves
The King and is a native of this country?

PAGE: He was killed in the battle of St. Quentin,
A Colonel of the Duke of Savoy's horse,
By name Alonzo Count of Henarez.

CARLOS:

(as he takes him by the hand and fixes his eye meaningfully
upon him)

The King gave you this letter?

PAGE: (hurt)   Gracious Prince,
How should I merit this distrust?

CARLOS: (reads the letter.)   "This key will open
The farther chambers of the Queen's pavilion.
The rearmost of them all adjoins on one side   1280
A private room to which the footfall of
A listening spy has yet to lose its way.
Here Love may make confession free and loud
Of what it has so long confided to
Mere signs. Requitement waits there for the timid,
And for the modest sufferer, reward."

          (awaking as though from bewilderment)

I am not dreaming—no, nor raving——this
Is my right arm—this is my sword—and these
Are written syllables. And it is true
And real. She loves me—loves me—yes, she does,   1290
She does love me!

          (rushing about the room beside himself,
          his arms in the air)

PAGE: Come then, my Prince, and I will take you there.

CARLOS: First let me come back to myself.—Do all

The terrors of this joy not tremble still
Within me? Have I hoped thus proudly? Have
I ever dared to dream of this? Where is
The man who learned so quickly to be God?—
Who was I, and who am I now? This is
Another heaven and another sun
From those that formerly were there.—She loves me!   1300
PAGE: (*about to lead him away*)
    Prince, here is not the place—Prince, you forget—
CARLOS: (*seized with a sudden numbness*)
    The King, my father!
                    (*He drops his arms, looks cautiously
                    around, and begins to get control of himself.*)
                            This is horrible—
Yes, quite right, friend. I thank you. I was not
Myself just now.—But it is horrible
That I must keep *that* silent, and wall up
So much of blessedness within this bosom.
                    (*taking the page by the hand and
                    leading him aside*)
What you have seen—you hear?—and not seen, let it
Be sunk within your bosom like a coffin.
Now go. I'll find my way there. Go. No one
Must meet us here. Go—
                    (*The page starts to go.*)
                            Wait! Wait! Listen to me!—   1310
(*The page comes back. Carlos lays his hand on his shoulder
    and looks earnestly and solemnly into his face.*)
You take a fearful secret with you, which
Like certain potent poisons, bursts asunder
The vessel which has served as its container.—
Be master of your features. Never let
Your head discover what your bosom guards.
Be like the dead mouthpiece that takes the sound
And gives it back but never hears itself.
You are a boy—continue to be such

And go on playing as the merry lad—
How well the clever writer understood   1320
The choosing of a messenger for love!
The King will never seek his adders *here*.
PAGE: And I, my Prince, I shall be proud to be
Aware I am one secret richer than
The King himself—
CARLOS: You vain and boyish fool,
That's just what you must tremble at.—If it
Should happen that we meet in public, you must
Approach me shyly, with submission. Never
Let vanity mislead you to sly hints,
Be the Infánt however gracious to you.   1330
You cannot sin, my son, more deeply than
By pleasing *me*.—Whatever information
You henceforth have for me, pronounce it never
In syllables, nor trust it to your lips;
Let your news never travel on the common
Highway of thoughts. You will speak rather with
The lashes of your eyes, your index finger;
And I shall listen with my gaze. The air,
The light about us, both are Philip's creatures;
Deaf walls themselves are in his pay.—Someone   1340
Is coming—
                (*The Queen's door opens and the Duke
                of Alba steps out.*)
                Go! Until we meet again!
PAGE: Take care, Prince, not to miss the proper room!
                (*Exit the page.*)
CARLOS: It is the Duke.—No, that is quite all right,
I'll find my way.
ALBA: (*intercepting him*) Two words, my gracious Prince.
CARLOS: Quite so—quite so—another time.
                (*He starts to go.*)
ALBA: The place
Seems frankly not the most appropriate.

Perhaps your royal Highness would be pleased
To grant me audience in your own room?

CARLOS: What for? That can be done right here.—But quickly,
Be brief—

ALBA: The thing that really brings me here   1350
Is to express a subject's dutiful
Thanks for the service that you know of.

CARLOS: Thanks?
To me? For what?—Thanks from the Duke of Alba?

ALBA: For scarcely had you left the Monarch's room
When the assignment was announced to me
To leave for Brussels.

CARLOS: Leave for Brussels! So!

ALBA: To what, my Prince, can I ascribe this, other
Than to your gracious intercession with
His Majesty the King?

CARLOS: To me?—To me
By no means whatsoever—not at all.   1360
You go—Then go with God!

ALBA: No more than this?
I am astounded.—Can your Highness have
No further mission for me into Flanders?

CARLOS: What further there?

ALBA: And yet but recently
It seemed as though those countries' fates required
Don Carlos's own presence there.

CARLOS: How so?
Oh, yes—quite right—that was before—that is
Quite properly the case, so much the better—

ALBA: I listen with astonishment—

CARLOS: (without irony)   You are
A famous general—who does not know that?   1370
Envy itself must swear to that. I—I
Am a young man. That's what the King thought too.
The King moreover is quite right, quite right.
I see that now, and I am satisfied,

And so enough of that. A prosperous journey!
Just now, as you can see, I simply cannot—
It happens I am somewhat busy now—
The rest tomorrow, or when you will, or else
When you come back from Brussels—

ALBA: How is that?

CARLOS:

(after a silence, when he sees that the Duke is still standing there)

You go at a good time of year.—The journey   1380
Goes through Milan, Lorraine, and Burgundy,
And Germany.—And Germany?—Quite right,
It *was* in Germany! They know you there!—
It is now April; May—June—by July,
Quite right, by early August at the latest
You will arrive in Brussels. O, I doubt not
We soon shall hear about your victories.
You will be able then to make yourself
Deserving of our gracious trust.

ALBA: *(pointedly)*   Will I,
"Crushed as I am by the awareness of   1390
My insignificance?"

CARLOS: *(after a silence, with dignity and pride)*
                    Duke, you are touchy,—
And rightly so. It was, I must admit,
Quite inconsiderate of me to take
Up arms against you which you are in no
Position to turn back on me.

ALBA: In no
Position?—

CARLOS: *(smiling and extending his hand to him)*
          What a shame I have no time now
To fight this worthy battle out with Alba.
Some other time—

ALBA: We are miscalculating,
Prince, in quite different ways. You, for example,

You see yourself advanced by twenty years,   1400
I see you younger to the same degree.
CARLOS: Well?
ALBA: It occurs to me how many nights
Spent with his lovely Portuguese, his spouse,—
Your mother, Prince,—the Monarch would have given
To purchase for his crown an arm like *this* one.
He may have realized quite clearly how
Much easier a thing it is to carry
A line of monarchs forward than a line
Of monarchies—how much more readily
The world can be provided with a king   1410
Than kings can be provided with a world.
CARLOS: Quite true! And yet, Duke Alba? nonetheless—
ALBA: And how much blood, blood of *your* people, had
To flow before two drops could make *you* King.
CARLOS: Quite true, by God,—and in two words you have
Compressed all that the pride of merit can
Oppose against the pride of fortune.—But
The application? Nonetheless, Duke Alba?
ALBA: Woe to the tender infant Majesty
That can mock at its nurse!How softly it   1420
May lay itself to sleep upon the downy
Pillows of our victories. Upon
The crown the pearls will gleam alone, but not
The wounds by which it was acquired.—This sword
Has written Spanish laws for foreign peoples,
Before the crucifix it blazed a path
With lightning, clove the bloody furrow for
The Faith's seed-grain upon this continent:
God set the course in Heaven, I on earth—
CARLOS: God or the Devil, it's all one! You were   1430
His own right arm. That I well know.—And now
No more of this. I beg you. I would gladly
Protect myself from certain memories.—
I do respect my father's choice. My father

Needs an Alba; *that* he needs this one
Is something which I do not envy him.
You are a great man.—That may well be so,
And I almost believe it. But, I fear,
You came a few millennia too soon.
An Alba, I should think, would be a man   1440
Who should come at the very end of time:
When the Titanic insolence of vice
Has worn out Heaven's patience, when the rich
Grain-harvest of misdeeds stands in full ear
And calling for a reaper without equal,
Then *you* would be in proper place.—My God,
My Paradise! My Flanders!—But I must
Not think of that now. Silence there. They say
You're taking a supply of sentences
Of death along, signed in advance? Your foresight   1450
Is admirable. This way you need not be
Afraid of any technical delays.—
How ill I understood your meaning, Father!
I blamed your hardness in refusing me
A mission where your Albas shine?—Ah, that
Was the beginning of respect on your part.
ALBA: Prince, that remark would merit—
CARLOS: (*flaring up*)   What?
ALBA: The Prince
In you shields you from *that*.
CARLOS: (*reaching for his sword*)   This calls for blood!—
Duke, draw your sword!
ALBA: (*coldly*)   Against whom?
CARLOS: (*pressing him urgently*)   Draw your sword,
And I will run you through.
ALBA: (*draws.*)   If you will have   1460
It so—
                    (*They fight.*)
        (*The Queen comes in fright from her room.*)
QUEEN: Drawn swords at my own threshhold!

(*to the Prince, indignantly and with imperious voice*)

Carlos!

CARLOS:

(*beside himself at sight of the Queen, drops his arms, stands motionless and senseless; then he rushes up to the Duke and kisses him.*)

Forgive me, Duke! Let all this be forgiven!

(*He throws himself wordless at the Queen's feet, then gets up quickly, and rushes away overcome.*)

ALBA:

(*who is standing there in astonishment, not taking his eyes from them*)

By God, but this is curious!—

QUEEN:

(*stands a few minutes uneasy and in doubt; then she walks slowly toward her room; at the door she turns around.*)

Duke Alba!

(*The Duke follows her into the room.*)

SCENE 3

A private apartment of the Princess of Eboli.
The Princess, beautifully but simply clad in an ideal style, is playing the lute and singing. Enter the Queen's page.

PRINCESS: (*jumps up quickly.*)

He's here!

PAGE: (*in haste*) Are you alone? I am amazed

To find he is not here yet; but he must

Appear at any moment.

PRINCESS: Must he? Well,

He *will* then—and the matter is decided—

PAGE: He follows on my heels.—My gracious Princess,

He is in love with you—in love, in love

As no one can be or has ever been.   1470
What a scene I witnessed!
PRINCESS: (*clasps him to her with impatience.*)
                  Tell me quickly!
You spoke with him? Be quick! What did he say?
How did he act? What were his very words?
He seemed embarrassed, seemed confused? Did he
Guess who the person was who sent the key?
Quick—or did he not guess? Did he not guess
Then, after all? or guess the wrong one?—Well?
You do not speak a single word in answer?
For shame, for shame! you never were so wooden,
Never so intolerably slow.   1480
PAGE: Most gracious Lady, may I get to speak?
I did deliver him both key and note
In the Queen's antechamber. He was startled
And looked at me when I let slip the word
A lady had despatched me.
PRINCESS: He was startled?
O very good! Go on, tell me the rest.
PAGE: I was about to say still more, when he
Turned pale and seized the letter from my hand,
Looked hard at me and said that he knew all.
He read the letter with confusion, then   1490
Began to tremble suddenly.
PRINCESS: Knew all?
That he knew all? Did he say that?
PAGE: And asked
Me three or four times whether you yourself
Had really given me the letter.
PRINCESS: I
Myself? Then he called me by name?
PAGE: By name?—
No, he did not call you by name.—There might,
He said, be spies in the vicinity
To hear and tattle to the King.

PRINCESS: (*surprised*)   Did he
   Say that?
PAGE: The King, he said, would set great store,
   Amazingly great store, especially great,   1500
   By getting information of this letter.
PRINCESS: The King? Can you have heard aright? The King?
   Did he use that precise expression?
PAGE: Yes.
   He said it was a secret fraught with danger
   And warned me to be very much on guard
   In word and gesture so the King might not
   Conceive the least suspicion.
PRINCESS: (*after some reflection, full of amazement*)
                           Everything
   Fits in—There is no other way—he must
   Know of that story.—Unbelievable!
   But who can have betrayed it to him?—Who?   1510
   I ask again—Who sees so sharp and deep
   Unless it is the falcon-eye of love?
   But do proceed, continue with your tale:
   He read the note—
PAGE: The note contained, he said,
   A happiness at which he had to tremble,
   He had not dared to dream of such a thing.
   Unfortunately the Duke came in the room,
   And that obliged us to—
PRINCESS: (*with irritation*)   What in the world
   Was the Duke doing there just then?—But where
   Can he be staying? Why does he delay?   1520
   Why does he not appear?—You see how falsely
   You were informed! How happy he might well
   Have been in this time it has taken you
   To tell me how much he wished to become so!
PAGE: The Duke, I am afraid—
PRINCESS: The Duke again?
   What does he matter *here*? What has my quiet

Happiness to do with that brave man?
He could have left him standing, sent him off—
Who in the world can not be gotten rid of?—
Indeed, your Prince knows love itself, it seems,   1530
As poorly as he knows the hearts of women.
He doesn't know what minutes are.—But quiet!
Someone is coming. Go! It is the Prince.
                    (*The Page hurries out.*)
Be off, be off!—Where did I put my lute?
He must come on me by surprise,—my singing
Must be the sign to him—
(*The Princess has thrown herself on a divan and is playing
     the lute.*
*Enter Carlos precipitately. He recognizes the Princess and
     stands as though struck by a thunderbolt.*)
CARLOS: My God!
Where am I?
PRINCESS: (*drops the lute. Going toward him*)
                    Ah, Prince Carlos? Yes, indeed!
CARLOS: Where am I? Monstrous treachery—I have
Missed the right room.
PRINCESS: How well Charles understands
The way of taking note of rooms where ladies   1540
Without attendants may be found.
CARLOS: Oh, Princess—
Forgive me, Princess—I—The antechamber,
I found it open.
PRINCESS: Is that possible?
And yet I fancy I myself had locked it.
CARLOS: You only fancy, fancy—but for certain
You are mistaken. You intended to,
I grant you, I believe you,—but not locked,
You did not lock it, surely not! I hear
The playing of a lute by someone—was
It not a lute?
                    (*as he looks around in doubt*)

Why yes! for there it is   1550
Still lying there—And God in Heaven knows
I love lute music to the point of madness.
I am all ears, I am myself no longer,
I rush into the room to look into
The sweet musician's eyes who touched me so
Divinely, cast a spell so mighty on me.
PRINCESS: A gracious curiosity, which you
Soon satisfied, as I might demonstrate.
                    (*after a silence, pointedly*)
I must esteem the modest man who will,
To save a woman from embarrassment,   1560
Enmesh himself in lies like these.
CARLOS: (*candidly*)   Oh, Princess,
I feel myself I am but making worse
What I seek to improve. Release me from
A role which I am absolutely hopeless
Of carrying through. You had come here to seek
A refuge from the world within this room.
Unheard by anyone, you wished to give
Yourself up to the quiet wishes of
Your heart. And I, Misfortune's son, appear;
Immediately this lovely dream is broken.—   1570
Therefore my suddenest departure shall—
                    (*He starts to leave.*)
PRINCESS: Prince, that was cruel.
CARLOS: Princess—I understand
What *this* glance in this room must signify
And for this virtuous embarrassment
I have respect. Woe to the man who is
Made brave at the sight of a woman's blush!
Courage fails in me when women tremble
Before me.
PRINCESS: Is it possible?—A conscience
Unparalleled for a young man and prince!
Yes, Prince,—now you must surely stay with me,   1580

I ask that now myself: before such virtue
The fears of any girl are calmed. But do you know
That your precipitate appearance here
Frightened me amid my favorite song?

> (*She leads him to the sofa and takes up
> her lute again.*)

Now I shall have to play the song all over
Again, Prince Carlos, and your punishment
Shall be to hear me play.

> (*He sits down, not entirely without
> constraint, next to the Princess.*)

CARLOS: A punishment
As much to be desired as was my crime.—
Indeed the purport was so welcome to me,
Was so divinely lovely, that I could   1590
Hear it—a third time.

PRINCESS: What? You heard it all?
That is abominable, Prince.—Love was
The subject of the song, as I recall?
And if I do not err, a happy love,—

No text more lovely on your lovely lips;
Yet said with less of truth and more of beauty.

PRINCESS: With less of truth?—You are in doubt of that?—

CARLOS: (*earnestly*)
I almost doubt if Carlos and the Princess
Of Eboli can ever understand
Each other when love is discussed.

> (*The Princess is startled; he notices it
> and continues with light gallantry.*)
>
>   For who,   1600

Who will believe it of these rosy cheeks
That passion rages in this bosom? Does
The Princess Eboli run any risk
Of sighing vainly and unheard? For love
Is known by him alone who loves past hope.

PRINCESS: (*with all her previous gaiety*)

Be quiet! That sounds frightful.—Actually
That fate would seem to be pursuing you
Before all others, most of all today.

        (taking his hand, with ingratiating interest)

Good Prince, you are not happy—you are grieving—
Yes, really grieving. Is it possible?   1610
Why should you grieve, Prince, with your evident
Vocation to the world's delights, with all
The gifts from lavishly bestowing Nature,
And all your claim upon the joys of life?
You—a great King's son and more besides,
Far more than that, endowed already from
Your princely cradle with such gifts as darken
The very radiance of your high rank?
You—who have bribed judges seated in
The whole strict court of ladies, ladies who   1620
Pass judgment, finally, without appeal,
Upon the worth of men and on men's fame?
And he who makes a conquest where he merely
Bestowed his notice, kindles fire where he
Remained quite cold, and where he wills to burn
Must sport with Paradises and make gifts
Of godlike happiness—the man whom Nature
Adorned to render thousands happy and
Gave like gifts but to *few*, should he be wretched
Himself?—O Heaven, you who gave him all,   1630
Why have you then denied him only eyes
With which to see his triumph?

CARLOS:

    (who all this time has been sunk in the deepest abstraction, is
       suddenly brought to himself by the silence of the Princess
       and leaps up.)

                            Excellent!

Incomparable, Princess. Please sing me
That passage through once more.

PRINCESS: *(looks at him in astonishment.)* Where have you been

All this time, Carlos?

CARLOS: (*jumps up.*)   Yes, by Heaven! You
Remind me in good time—I must, I must
Be gone—I must be off in haste.

PRINCESS: (*holds him back.*)   Where to?

CARLOS: (*in terrible anxiety*)   Down to
The open air.—Do not detain me—Princess,
I feel as though the world were bursting forth
In smoke and flames behind me—

PRINCESS: (*holds him back by force.*) What is wrong?   1640
Whence comes this strange unnatural behavior?
(*Carlos stops and becomes pensive. She seizes this moment to
draw him down beside her on the sofa.*)
You need to rest, dear Charles.—Your blood is now
In tumult.—Come, sit down beside me here.—
Away with these black fever-fantasies!
If you inquire quite frankly of yourself,
Does this head know what burdens this heart down?
And even if it did know, is there no one
Of all the knights at court not one, not one
Of all the ladies,—not a single one
Worthy of working your recovery,   1650
Of understanding you?

CARLOS: (*desultorily, without thinking*)
                    Perhaps the Princess
Of Eboli—

PRINCESS: (*joyously, quickly*)
            Indeed?

CARLOS: Give me a letter
To recommend me—a petition to
My father. Give me that. They say your word
Counts heavily with him.

PRINCESS: Who says so? (Ha!
So *that* suspicion made you mute!)

CARLOS: Already
The story is about, it seems. I have

The sudden thought of going to Brabant
In order to—well, just to win my spurs.
My father does not wish it—My good father   1660
Fears that, if I were in command of armies—
My singing voice might suffer by it.

PRINCESS: Carlos,
You're playing false. Confess that in this serpent
Wriggling you are trying to evade me.
Look at me now, deceiver, eye to eye!
A man who merely dreams of knightly deeds—
Will he—confess!—will he descend so low
That he will covetously filch ribbons which
May have been lost by ladies and—forgive me—
*(as she snatches away his shirt-frill with a swift movement of
    her finger and seizes a ribbon which is hidden there)*
Preserve them then as preciously as this?   1670

CARLOS: *(falling back in surprise)*
No, Princess,—you are going too far.—I am
Betrayed. But no one is deceiving you.—
You are allied with spirits and with demons.

PRINCESS: You seem to be amazed at this? At this?
What will you wager, Prince, that I can call
Back stories to your heart, yes, stories which—
But put me to the test, interrogate me.
If even whims of mood, a syllable
Breathed with distortion to the air, a smile
Wiped out again with sudden earnestness,   1680
If even looks and gestures when your soul
Was far away did not escape me, be
The judge of whether I did understand
The things which you wished to be understood.

CARLOS: Now that is risking much indeed.—The wager
Is taken, Princess. You are promising
Me revelations inside my own heart
That I was never conscious of.

PRINCESS: *(somewhat offended and seriously)* What, never?

Reflect with better care. Just look about you.—
This room is not one of the Queen's rooms where   1690
A slight deception was in any case
Considered fit for praise.—But you are startled?
You are all ardor suddenly?—O, really,
Who would be so presumptuous or so cunning,
Or have the idle time to spy on Carlos
When Carlos thinks himself unspied on?—Who
Observed how at the last court ball he left
The Queen, his lady, standing in the dance
And forced his way between the nearest couple
To give his hand to Princess Eboli   1700
Instead of to his royal dancing partner?
An error, Prince, of which the Monarch even
Took notice, for he had just then come in!

CARLOS: (*with a smile of irony*)
Ah, even he? In very truth, good Princess,
That was not specially on *his account*.

PRINCESS: No more than was that scene in the court chapel
Of which Prince Carlos now has probably
No recollection. Lost in prayer you lay
Before the feet of the Most Holy Virgin
When suddenly—Could you prevent it?—at   1710
Your back the gowns of certain ladies rustled.
And then Don Philip's hero-hearted son
Began to tremble like a heretic
Beholding Holy Mass; on his pale lips
His desecrated prayer died out—Caught up
In passion's frenzied whirl—it was a farce
To stir one's pity, Prince—you seize the hand,
The cold and sacred hand of God's own Mother
And on the marble rain down fiery kisses.

CARLOS: You wrong me, Princess. That was piety.   1720

PRINCESS: Yes, then there is another thing, Prince.—That
Was merely fear of losing, I suppose,
That time when Carlos sat with me and with

The Queen at cards and with amazing deftness
Stole that glove from me—
            (*Carlos jumps up in consternation.*)
                 which he was nice
Enough, indeed, directly afterwards
To play instead of leading with a card.

CARLOS: O God—God—God! What thing did I commit then?

PRINCESS: Why, nothing that you will revoke, I trust.
How startled and how glad I was to find   1730
Most unexpectedly a note which you
Had managed to conceal inside that glove.
It was the most affecting ballad, Prince,
That—

CARLOS: (*interrupting her quickly*)
         Poetry!—and nothing more.—My brain
Sends up at times extraordinary bubbles
That burst as suddenly as they arise.
It was no more than that. Let's speak no more
Of that.

PRINCESS: (*walking away from him in astonishment and observing him for a time from a distance*)
         I am used up—all my attempts
Glide off this serpent-slippery curious fellow.
            (*She is silent for a few instants.*)
Yet?—Could it be immense male vanity   1740
Which merely to derive more sweet delight
Is using fatuousness as its disguise?
(*She approaches the Prince again and observes him dubiously.*)
Will you at last instruct me, Prince—I stand
Before a cupboard locked by magic where
My every key deceives my expectations.

CARLOS: As *I* stand before *you*.
(*She leaves him abruptly, walks silently up and down the room several times, and seems to be pondering something of importance. Finally after a long pause, earnestly and solemnly*)

PRINCESS: So be it then—
I must bring myself to the point of speaking.
I choose you as my judge. You are a noble
Human being—man, and prince, and knight.
I cast myself upon your bosom. You   1750
Will rescue me, Prince, and, where I am lost
Beyond all rescue, weep with pity for me.
            (*The Prince moves nearer with expectant
                    compassionate astonishment.*)
An insolent favorite of the Monarch seeks
My hand—Rui Gomez, the Count of Silva—
The King desires, the bargain is already
Made up, to sell me to this creature.
CARLOS: (*vehemently moved*)   Sell?
And sell again? And once again sold by
That famous bargainer of southern Europe?
PRINCESS: No, first hear all of it. Not satisfied
With sacrificing me to politics,   1760
My innocence is also being tempted—
There! Here! This letter will unmask that saint.
(*Carlos takes the paper and hangs, full of impatience, on her
        story without taking time to read it.*)
Prince, where shall I find rescue? Until now
It was my pride that was my virtue's shield;
But now at last—
CARLOS: At last you fell? You fell?
No, no! in Heaven's name!
PRINCESS: (*proudly and nobly*) But through whose fault?
O wretched sophistry! How weak of these
Strong spirits to esteem a woman's favor
And all the happiness of love as equal
To wares for which one bids at sale. It is   1770
The only thing upon this round of earth
That tolerates no buyer but itself.
Love only is the price of love. It is
The priceless diamond which I must *give*

Or else, forever unenjoyed, must *bury*—
Like that great merchant who, unmoved by all
The proffered gold of the Rialto, and
In scorn of kings, cast his pearl back into
The wealthy sea, too proud to part with it
For less than its true worth.

CARLOS: (Now by the God   1780
Of wonders—she is beautiful, this woman!)

PRINCESS: Call it whim—or vanity: no matter.
I do not parcel out my joys. For that
One man whom I have chosen for myself
I will surrender everything. I give
But *once,* but then eternally. One man
Alone will be made happy by my love,
But that one shall be made a god by it.
Two souls' enraptured harmony—a kiss—
The trysting-hour's riot of delights—   1790
Beauty's high celestial magic force
Are sister colors of a single ray,
Are merely petals of a single flower.
Should I—mad woman!—give away one petal
Plucked from the lovely chalice of that flower?
Or mutilate the lofty majesty
Of woman, the great masterpiece of godhead,
To gratify the evening of a rake?

CARLOS: (Incredible! Madrid possessed a girl
Like this, and I—I only find it out   1800
Today?)

PRINCESS: I should long since have left this court,
And left the world as well; I should have buried
Myself in sacred walls; and yet there is
One single bond remaining still, a bond
That binds me utterly unto this world.—
Perhaps a phantom, but so dear to me!
I love, and am—not loved.

CARLOS: (*going toward her, full of ardor*)
                            Oh, but you are!
As truly as there dwells a God in Heaven.
I swear you are, unutterably.
PRINCESS: You swear?
You? O that was my angel's voice! Yes, if   1810
You really swear, Charles, then I will believe you,
For then I am.
CARLOS: (*Who takes her, all tenderness, into his arms*)
                          My sweet, true-hearted girl!
You creature who should be adored!—I stand
All ears—all eyes—all rapture—all amazement.—
Who ever could have looked upon you, who
Beneath this heaven could have looked upon you
And made his boast—that he had never loved?—
And yet here at King Philip's court? What, what,
O lovely angel, are you doing here?
With priests and all the monkish tribe? This is   1820
No climate for such flowers!—Would they like
To pick them? Would they like—I can imagine—
But no! As surely as I breathe, I'll put
My arm around you, and safe in my arms
I'll carry you through devil-teeming hell!
Yes!—Let me be your angel—
PRINCESS: (*with the full glance of love*) O my Carlos!
How little did I know you! O how richly
And boundlessly your noble heart rewards
The heavy toil to comprehend it!
                    (*She takes his hand and starts to kiss it.*)
CARLOS: Princess,
Where are you now?
PRINCESS: (*with delicacy and grace, as she stares at his hand*)
                        How beautiful this hand is!   1830
How rich it is!—This hand, Prince, still has to
Bestow two precious gifts—a diadem

And Carlos's own heart—and both perhaps
Upon a single mortal?—Only one?
A great and godlike gift!—Almost too great
For one mere mortal woman!—What, Prince, if
You should decide on a division of them?
Queens love but poorly—and a woman who
Can love is poor at understanding crowns:
Hence better, Prince, that you divide, and now,   1840
At once.—Or can you have already done so?
You really have? Oh then so much the better!
And do I know the happy one?

CARLOS: You shall.
To you, dear girl, I will reveal myself—
To innocence, to Nature undefiled
And pure, I will reveal myself. You are
The worthiest, the first, the only one
At court who fully understands my soul.—
So—I will not deny—I am in love!

PRINCESS: Confession has become so hard for you,   1850
You wicked man? Would I be pitiable
Because you found me worthy of your love?

CARLOS: *(startled)*
What? What was that?

PRINCESS: To play a game like this
With me! O really, Prince, that was not nice.
And even to deny the key!

CARLOS: Key! Key!
                    (after gloomy meditation)
So—that was it.—I see now—O my God!
                    *(His knees falter, he steadies himself
                    against a chair and covers his face.)*
                    *(A long silence on both sides. The
                    Princess screams and falls.)*

PRINCESS: Abominable! What have I done!

CARLOS:
    (straightening up, in an outburst of the most vehement grief)

                                   Cast down
So far from all my heavens!—This is ghastly!
PRINCESS: (*burying her face in the cushion*)
    My God in Heaven, what have I discovered?
CARLOS: (*on his knees before her*)
    I am not guilty, Princess—passion—some   1860
    Unfortunate misunderstanding—but
    I swear I am not guilty.
PRINCESS: (*thrusting him away*)   In God's name,
    Out of my sight—
CARLOS: O never! Leave you now
    When you are in this frightful state of shock?
PRINCESS: (*pushing him away by force*)
    From magnanimity, from pity, out of
    My sight!—Or do you want to murder me?
    I hate the sight of you!
                    (*Carlos starts to go.*)
                     But give me back
    My letter and my key. Where did you put
    The other letter?
CARLOS: Other letter? Which?
    What other one?
PRINCESS: The letter from the King.   1870
CARLOS: (*shuddering*)
    From *whom?*
PRINCESS: The one you took from me before.
CARLOS: And from the King? To whom? To you?
PRINCESS: O Heaven!
    How horribly I have ensnared myself!
    The letter. I must have it back. Just hand
    It over!
CARLOS: Letters from the King, to you?
PRINCESS: That letter! In the name of all the saints!
CARLOS: The one which would unmask a certain saint—
    This one?
PRINCESS: I am undone!—O give it to me!

CARLOS: This letter—
PRINCESS: *(wringing her hands in despair)*
                    What, rash woman, have I done!
CARLOS: This letter—it came from the King?—Yes, Princess,   1880
  This does change everything all of a sudden—
  This is
                    (holding the letter aloft in exultation)
                a priceless—weighty—precious letter,
  Which all of Philip's crowns together are
  Too light, too trivial to redeem.—*This* letter
  I shall keep.
                        (He leaves.)
PRINCESS: *(throwing herself in his path)*
                    Great God! I am destroyed!
      *(She stands still dazed, aghast; after he has gone she hurries
          after him and tries to call him back.)*
  A word yet, Prince. Prince, listen to me.—He
  Is gone! Now this yet! He despises me.—
  And here I stand in frightful loneliness—
  Rejected—cast aside—
                    (She sinks down on a chair. After a pause)
                        No, just displaced,
  Just forced out by a rival. For he is   1890
  In love. No doubt about it. He himself
  Confessed it. But *who* is the happy one?
  This much is clear—he loves where he should not.
  He fears discovery. His passion creeps
  Away in hiding from the King.—But why
  From him, who wished it most?—Or is it not
  The father that he fears so in his father?
  Just when the King's unchaste designs became
  Apparent to him,—then his glance exulted,
  He gloated like a happy man. . . How does   1900
  It happen his stern virtue fell mute then?
  Precisely then?—What can he do about it,
  Or stand to gain, in case the King deceives

The Queen—
  (*She stops suddenly, surprised by an idea.—At the same
  time she snatches from her bosom the ribbon which
  Carlos gave her, looks at it quickly, and recognizes it.*)
Now at long last, now, now—Where were my wits?
My eyes are opened now.—They had been long
In love before the King selected her.
Not once without me did the Prince see *her.*—
So *she* was meant where I believed myself
So warmly, truly, boundlessly adored?   1910
O a deception without parallel!
And I myself betrayed my weakness to her—
                    (*silence*)
To think that he should love beyond all hope!
That I can not believe.—A hopeless love
Cannot survive in such a battle. Gorging
Where earth's most glorious monarch starves unheard,
A sacrifice like that is never made
By hopeless love. How ardent was his kiss!
How tenderly, how tenderly he clasped
Me to his throbbing heart!—A test almost   1920
Too bold for his romantic constancy
That he claims unrequited.—He accepts
The key, which, as he has convinced himself,
The Queen has sent to him—he puts his faith in
This giant step of love—and actually
Comes, comes!—He credits Philip's wife with this
Insane decision—How can he do that
If mighty trials do not lift his spirits?
It stands revealed. She loves. He is requited!
By Heaven, but that saint knows what love is!   1930
How subtle of her! . . . I, for my part, trembled
Before the sublime bugbear of that virtue.
A loftier being towers at my side
And in its splendor my light dies. I grudged
Her beauty its exalted calm untroubled

By any passions known to mortal natures.
That calm was mere illusion then? Did she
Intend to revel at both tables? Make
Display of god-like seeming virtue and
Yet simultaneously make bold to eat   1940
The secret raptures of depravity?
Could she do that? And should the false dissembler
Succeed there unavenged? and unavenged
Because no one would challenge her to vengeance?—
By Heaven, no!—I worshiped her.—This calls
For vengeance! Let the King know his betrayal—
The King?
                    (after some reflection)
          Yes, there's a way to reach his ear.
                    (She leaves.)

SCENE 4

A room in the royal palace.
The Duke of Alba. Father Domingo.

DOMINGO: What did you wish to tell me?
ALBA: An important
    Discovery that I made today, which I
    Would like to have elucidated.
DOMINGO: What   1950
    Discovery? What is it you mean?
ALBA: Prince Carlos
    And I this noon encountered one another
    In the Queen's antechamber. I receive
    An insult. Both of us grow hot. The quarrel
    Gets somewhat loud. We both reach for our swords.
    At the sound of the fray the Queen then opens
    Her chamber, throws herself between us, and
    With one glance of despotic intimacy

Looks at the Prince.—It was a single glance—
Then his arm freezes—he flies to my neck—   1960
I feel a burning kiss—and he has vanished.
DOMINGO: (*after some silence*)
What you tell me is most suspicious.—Duke,
You make me think of something—Similar
Thoughts, I confess, have long since had their growth
Within my heart.—I fled those dreams—I have
Confided them to no one yet. There are
Swords of a double edge, uncertain friends—
I fear these. Hard to differentiate
Are human beings, harder still to fathom.
Words indiscreetly dropped are confidants   1970
Who are offended.—So I hid my secret
Until the course of time brought it to light.
Performing certain services for kings
Is risky, Duke,—a boldly ventured shot
Which, if it fails the target, ricochets
Back on the marksman. I could swear to what
I say, upon the Host—but all the same,
Eye-witness evidence, a word caught by
The ear, a sheet of paper tips the scales
More than my vividest impression.—Damn   1980
The fact we stand on Spanish soil!
ALBA: Why not
Stand on this soil?
DOMINGO: At any other court
A passion can forget itself. But here
It is admonished by our fretful laws.
The Queens of Spain do find it difficult
To sin—I am convinced—unfortunately,
However, only *there*—just *there,* where we
Would have most luck to take them by surprise.
ALBA: Hear me further.—Carlos went today
Before the King. The audience took an hour.   1990
He asked for the administration of

The Netherlands. And loud and fervently
He asked; I heard it in the study. When
I met him at the door, his eyes were red
From weeping. Yet by noontime he appeared
With looks of triumph on his face. He is
Delighted that the King has chosen me.
He thanks me for it. Things stand otherwise,
Says he, and better. He never could dissemble.
What sense shall I make of these contradictions?   2000
The Prince is jubilant at being slighted,
And I receive a favor from the King
With all the ear-marks of his anger!—What
Am I to think? My newest dignity
Bears more resemblance to a banishment
Than to an honor.

DOMINGO: Have things gone that far?
As far as that? A single moment has
Destroyed what we have taken years to build?—
And you so calm? so passive?—Do you know
This youth? And have you any notion of   2010
What lies in store for us when he gets power?—
The Prince—I am no enemy of his.
But other cares gnaw at my rest, cares for
The throne, for God, and for the Church.—The Prince
(I know him—I can see right through his soul)
He entertains the monstrous scheme—Toledo—
The frenzied scheme of being ruler and
Of making do without our Holy Faith.—
His heart is all afire for a new virtue
Which, proud, assured, sufficient to itself,   2020
Does not intend to beg of any Faith.—
He *thinks!* His head is burning with an odd
Delusion—he respects mankind.—Duke, is he
A fit man to become our King?

ALBA: Mere notions!
What else? Perhaps his youthful pride as well,

Which may aspire to play a role.—But has
He any other choice? All that will pass
Once his turn has arrived to take command.
DOMINGO: I doubt it.—He is proud of freedom and
Unused to that control which one must yield to   2030
If one would buy control of others.—Is he
Fit for our throne? His daring Titan spirit
Will kick the traces of our statecraft over.
I have tried to blunt that rebel spirit
In vain amid these times of luxury.
He has withstood the trial.—Fearful is
That spirit in that body.—And then Philip
Is turning sixty years of age.
ALBA: Your vision
Looks far ahead.
DOMINGO: He and the Queen are one.
In both their bosoms lurks, as yet concealed,   2040
The poison of the innovators; all
Too soon, if it gains ground, it will engulf
The throne. I know this Valois.—We may fear
The total vengeance of this silent foe
If Philip lets himself be weak. Luck still
Is for us. Let us take preventive measures.
Let both of them fall in one snare.—Right now
A hint like this suggested to the King,
No matter whether proven or unproven,—
Much will be gained if he but wavers. We   2050
Ourselves both have no doubts. To one convinced
Convincing is not difficult. We can
Not help discovering still more if we
Are sure beforehand that we must discover.
ALBA: But now the most important of all questions!
Which one will take it on himself to tell
The King?
DOMINGO: Not you, nor I. Now let me tell
You how long since, while full of its great plan,

My quiet zeal has labored toward its goal.
To round out our alliance we still lack   2060
The third and most important party.—Now,
The King loves Princess Eboli. I foster
This passion which is useful to my wishes.
I am his go-between.—I shall apprise
Her of our plan.—In this young lady, if
My project is successful, you shall see
An ally and a queen will blossom for us.
She summoned me into this room herself
Just now. I have great hopes.—A Spanish girl
May snap those Valois fleurs-de-lys right off   2070
Perhaps within a single midnight.

ALBA: What!
Can it be true what I just heard?—By Heaven,
This takes me by surprise! Yes, that stroke does it!
Dominican, I must admire you. Now
Our game is won—

DOMINGO: Be quiet! Who is coming?
It's she—it's she herself.

ALBA: I will be in
The next room if—

DOMINGO: Quite right. I'll call you.
                    (*Exit the Duke of Alba. Enter the*
                              Princess.)
                                               At
Your orders, gracious Princess.

PRINCESS: (*looking curiously after the Duke*) Are we not
Entirely by ourselves? You have, I see,
Another witness with you?

DOMINGO: What?

PRINCESS: Who was it   2080
Who went away from you just now?

DOMINGO: The Duke
Of Alba, gracious Princess, who is asking
Permission after me to be admitted.

PRINCESS: The Duke of Alba? What does he want? What
Can he be looking for? Can you perhaps
Inform me?
DOMINGO: I? Before I even know
What meaningful occurrence has brought me
The long withheld good fortune of approaching
The Princess Eboli again?
                    (*a pause while he awaits her reply*)
                         Can it
Be that some circumstance has come about   2090
At last that favors what the King desires?
Or have I with good reason hoped that better
Reflection reconciles you to an offer
Which only self-will and caprice rejected?
I come now full of expectation—
PRINCESS: Did
You give the King my last reply?
DOMINGO: I was
Postponing dealing him that mortal wound.
There still is time, most gracious Princess, yet.
It rests with you to soften it.
PRINCESS: Inform
The King I am expecting him.
DOMINGO: May I   2100
Accept this as the truth, my lovely Princess?
PRINCESS: Well, surely not as jest? Good Lord! You make
Me quite uneasy—What? What have I done
That even you—that you yourself turn pale?
DOMINGO: Princess, this is so surprising—I
Can hardly grasp it—
PRINCESS: Worthy Sir, you are not
Supposed to do so. Not for all the world's
Possessions would I have you understand it.
Let it suffice you that it is so. Spare
Yourelf the effort of discerning whose   2110
Persuasion you need thank for this new turn.

I will add for your consolation: *You*
Have no part in this sin. Nor has the Church,
Indeed; although you proved to me that there
Were cases possible in which the Church
Might even use the *bodies* of its youthful
Daughters for its higher purposes.
It has no part in this.—Such pious grounds
As these, most worthy Sir, are much too high
For me—

DOMINGO: I would withdraw them gladly, Princess,   2120
As soon as they became superfluous.

PRINCESS: Request the Monarch in my name not to
Misjudge my motives in this undertaking.
I still am what I was before. However,
The situation meanwhile has been altered.
When I rejected his proposal with
Such indignation, I thought he was happy
In the possession of his lovely Queen—
And thought that loyal spouse was worthy of
My sacrifice. So I thought then—then. But   2130
Now I know better.

DOMINGO: Princess, further, further.
We understand each other.

PRINCESS: It suffices
She has been caught. I shall spare her no longer.
The crafty cheat has now been caught. She has
Betrayed the King and all of Spain and me.
She is in love. I know she is in love.
I'll bring proof of it as shall make her tremble.
The King has been betrayed—but, by the Lord!
He shall not be so unavenged. That mask
Of superhuman, sublime resignation,   2140
I'll tear it off from her so all the world
Shall recognize the sinner's brow. It will
Cost me a monstrous price, but—that delights me,
That is my triumph—but it will cost *her*

A greater one.

DOMINGO: Now everything is ripe.
Allow me, I shall summon in the Duke.
                    (*He goes out.*)

PRINCESS: (*astonished*)
What is this?
                (*Reenter Domingo leading the Duke.*)

DOMINGO: Our intelligence, Duke Alba,
Arrives too late. The Princess Eboli
Reveals a secret to us which she should
Have learned from us.

ALBA: My visit then will be   2150
Just that much less astonishing to her.
I do not trust *my* eyes. Discoveries
Of this sort do require a woman's vision.

PRINCESS: You talk about discoveries?—

DOMINGO: We would,
Most gracious Princess, like to know what place,
What more convenient time you—

PRINCESS: That as well!
I shall expect you by tomorrow noon.
I have my reasons why this guilty secret
Should not be hidden any longer—should
Not any more be withheld from the King.   2160

ALBA: This was the thing that brought me here. The Monarch
Must know of this immediately. And, Princess,
He must do so through you, through you. Whom else,
Whom should he sooner trust than the severe
And vigilant companion of his wife?

DOMINGO: Whom more than you, who, when she so desires,
Can have unlimited control of him?

ALBA: I am the sworn foe of the Prince.

DOMINGO: The same
Thing is assumed in my case usually.
The Princess Eboli is free. Where *we*   2170
Are forced to silence, duties must compel you

To speak, the duties of your charge. The King
Will not escape us if your hints impress him,
And we shall then complete the work.
ALBA: But this
Must be done soon, right now, in fact. Each moment
Is precious. Any hour now can bring me
The orders for departure—
DOMINGO: (turning, after some reflection, to the Princess)
                          If some letters
Could be discovered? Letters, to be sure,
From the Infánte, intercepted, would
Have their effect here.—Let me see—Do you?—   2180
Yes, you do sleep—as I remember—in
The same room with the Queen?
PRINCESS: The one
Right next to that.—But what is that to me?
DOMINGO: If someone good at locks . . .—Have you observed
In what place she habitually keeps
Her jewel-casket key?
PRINCESS: (pondering)   That could well lead
To something—Yes—It would be possible
To find the key, I think—
DOMINGO: Now letters call
For bearers——The Queen's retinue is large——
If one could only find some clue——Gold can,   2190
Of course, do much—
ALBA: Has no one ever noticed
Whether the Infánt has intimates?
DOMINGO: Not one, not one in all Madrid.
ALBA: That's odd.
DOMINGO: On that point you may trust me; he despises
The entire court; I have my proofs of that.
ALBA: And yet? It just occurs to me, as I
Came out of the apartment of the Queen,
The Prince was standing with one of her pages;

They were conversing secretly—
PRINCESS: *(quickly interrupting)* Oh no!
No, that was—that was something else.
DOMINGO: Can we   2200
Be sure of that?—The circumstance is suspect—
                    (to the Duke)
And did you know the page?
PRINCESS: Some childish nonsense!
What else can it have been? Let it suffice
I know that.—So then, we shall meet again
Before I see the King.—And meanwhile much
May be discovered.
DOMINGO: *(taking her aside)* And the Monarch may
Have hopes? I may inform him? Certainly?
And what delightful hour will bring for him
Fulfillment of his wishes? That as well?
PRINCESS: A few days hence I shall take sick; I shall   2210
Be separated from the person of
The Queen—that is court custom, as you know.
I shall remain then in my room.
DOMINGO: A fine
Idea. Our great game is won. Let all
The Queens be challenged in defiance—
PRINCESS: Hark!
They're asking for me—I am wanted by
The Queen. Until we meet again.
                    (She hurries away.)
DOMINGO: *(after a pause during which his eyes have
    followed the Princess)*
DOMINGO: Duke, with
These roses—and your battles—
ALBA: And your God—
I wait the lightning that can strike us down!

                    (Exeunt.)

SCENE 5

In a Carthusian monastery. [*Two days later*]
Don Carlos. The Prior.

CARLOS: (*to the Prior and he comes in*)
     Already been and left then?—I am sorry.   2220
PRIOR: It was no less than the third time this morning.
     He left an hour ago—
CARLOS: He will be back
     Again, however? Did he leave no message?
PRIOR: By noon, he promised.
CARLOS: (*at a window, surveying the landscape*)
                              I observe your cloister
     Stands far back from the highway.—Yonder one
     Can even see the towers of Madrid.—
     And there flows the Manzanares.—The landscape
     Is just as I would have it.—Everything
     Is quiet as a secret here.
PRIOR: Like entrance
     Into the other life.
CARLOS: To your uprightness   2230
     I have entrusted, venerable Sir,
     My holiest, most precious thing. No mortal
     Must know or even guess to *whom* I spoke here,
     Or even *that* I spoke *in secret*. I
     Have very weighty reasons to deny
     Before the entire world the man whom I
     Am waiting for; therefore I chose this cloister.
     We *are* safe here from traitors and surprise?
     You still remember what you swore to me?
PRIOR: Sir, let us trust each other. The suspicion   2240
     Of Kings will not go searching through these *graves*.
     The ear of curiosity is laid
     To doors of happiness and passion only.

The world ends at these walls.

CARLOS: Perhaps you think
Behind this caution and this fear a guilty
Conscience may be crouching hidden?

PRIOR: I
Think nothing.

CARLOS: You are wrong there, pious Father,
You are entirely wrong. My secret trembles
In men's sight but not in the sight of God.

PRIOR: My son, that troubles us but little. Open   2250
To crime and innocence alike this place
Of refuge stands. If what you have in mind
Be good or evil, just or wicked,—that
You must determine in your heart.

CARLOS: *(with warmth)*   What we
Keep secret here can not disgrace your God.
It is His own most noble work.—To you,
To you I can reveal it.

PRIOR: To what end?
Spare me the telling rather, Prince. The world
And all its instruments has long since lain
Sealed up and ready for that mighty journey.   2260
Why open it again for this brief time
Before departure?—It is little that
One needs for blessedness.—The bell for Hora
Is ringing. I must go to say my prayers.
    *(Exit the Prior. Enter the Marquis
    of Posa.)*

CARLOS: Ah, finally and at long last we—

MARQUIS: What
A trial of a friend's impatience! Twice
The sun has risen, twice the sun has set
Since the fate of my Carlos was decided,
And not till now, till now will I hear of it.—
Tell me, are you reconciled?

CARLOS: Who?

MARQUIS: Why,   2270
  You and King Philip; and has a decision
  Been reached on Flanders?
CARLOS: That the Duke rides there
  Tomorrow, that much is decided, yes.
MARQUIS: That cannot be. Is all Madrid deceived?
  They say you had a private audience.
  The King—
CARLOS: Remained unmoved. We are divided
  For good, more than we ever were—
MARQUIS: You will
  Not go to Flanders?
CARLOS: No! No! No!
MARQUIS: My hopes!
CARLOS: That by the way. O Roderick, since we
  Last saw each other, what I have lived through!   2280
  But first of all now your advice! I must
  See her—
MARQUIS: Your mother?—No!—What for?
CARLOS: There is
  Some hope for me—Do you turn pale? Be still.
  I must and shall be happy—But of that
  Another time. Right now devise means for
  My seeing her—
MARQUIS: What does this mean? What is
  This newest fever dream based on?
CARLOS: No dream!
  No, by the wondrous God!—The truth, the truth!
    (*taking out the King's letter to*
      the Princess Eboli)
  It is contained in this important paper!
  The Queen is *free;* before the eyes of men,   2290
  And free as well before the eyes of Heaven.
  Read this and cease to be astounded.
MARQUIS: What?

What do I see? The Monarch's own handwriting?
                (after he has read it)
Whom was this letter sent to?
CARLOS: To the Princess
  Of Eboli.—Day before yesterday
  One of the pages of the Queen brought me
  A letter and a key from hands unknown.
  A private room was designated in
  The left wing of the palace where the Queen lives
  And where a lady was expecting me   2300
  With whom I long had been in love. I took
  The hint at once and followed—
MARQUIS: Madman! Followed?
CARLOS: I did not recognize the writing—I
  Knew only one such lady. Who but *she*
  Would ever think she was adored by Carlos?
  Full of sweet rapture I flew to the place;
  A voice divinely singing toward me from
  Within the room performed the service of
  A guide—I opened up the chamber door—
  And whom do I discover?—Guess my horror!   2310
MARQUIS: O, I guess everything.
CARLOS: I would have been
  Lost, Roderick, beyond all rescue, had I
  Not fallen into the hands of an angel.
  Unfortunate coincidence! Misled
  By the uncautious language of my glances,
  She had surrendered to the sweet illusion
  She was herself the idol of those glances.
  Touched by the silent sorrows of my soul,
  Her soft heart recklessly-magnanimously
  Had brought itself to give me love in turn.   2320
  Respect seemed to be forcing me to silence;
  Then she was bold enough to break it—Open
  To me her great soul lay—

MARQUIS: Are you so calm
   In telling this?—The Princess Eboli
   Saw through you. Not a doubt of it, she pierced
   Down to the inmost secret of your love.
   You have hurt her severely. She controls
   The King.
CARLOS: (confidently) But she is virtuous.
MARQUIS: She is so
   From the self-interest of love.—This virtue,
   I gravely fear I know its kind—how little   2330
   It measures up to that ideal which
   From the maternal seed-ground of the soul,
   Wherein it was conceived in lovely grace,
   Grows up of its free will and, without tending
   By gardners, bears abundant bloom! This is
   An alien bough which in harsh latitudes
   Has flowered with a counterfeited South;
   Or call it rearing, rule of conduct, what
   You will, this is an *innocence acquired*,
   From hot blood wrested by craft and hard struggle   2340
   And conscientiously and carefully
   Ascribed to Heaven which requires it and
   Rewards it. Think it over. Will she ever
   Be able to forgive the Queen when some
   Man has passed over her own hard-won virtue
   Just so that he in turn may be consumed
   With hopeless passion for Don Philip's wife?
CARLOS: You know the Princess in such fine detail?
MARQUIS: Of course not. I have scarcely seen her twice.
   But let me tell you just one word. I fancied   2350
   She skillfully avoided vice's pitfalls
   And was completely *conscious* of her virtue.
   But then I also saw the Queen—O Charles!
   How different utterly what I saw there!
   In quiet glory native to her, with
   Untroubled lightness, unacquainted with

Pedantic calculation of decorum,
Removed from brashness and from fear alike,
With firm heroic tread she walks along
The narrow middle path of *rectitude,*   2360
Not knowing she compels one's adoration
Where she has never dreamed of self-approval.
Now does my Charles still recognize here in
This mirror his own Eboli?—The Princess
Stood firm because she was in love; love was
A literal condition on her virtue.
You left it unrequited:—it will fall.

CARLOS: *(with some vehemence)*
No! No!

        (after pacing excitedly back and forth)
        I tell you, No!—If Roderick
But knew how excellently it became him
To rob his Charles of the most godlike of   2370
His blisses, faith in human excellence!

MARQUIS: Do I deserve that?—No, my soul's Beloved,
By God in Heaven, that I would not do!—
This Eboli—she would have been an angel,
And reverently, like you, I would now cast
Myself before her glory, had she not—
Found out your secret.

CARLOS: See how vain your fear is!
Are there any other proofs for it
Than those that put themselves to shame? Will she
Pay with her honor for the melancholy   2380
Satisfaction of revenge?

MARQUIS: O many
Have sacrificed themselves to shame in order
To cancel out a blush.

CARLOS: *(standing up with vehemence)*
              Oh no, that is
Too harsh, too cruel. She is proud and noble;
I know her and I have no fears. You seek

In vain to put my fears to flight in terror.
I shall speak with my mother.

MARQUIS: Now? What for?

CARLOS: I have now nothing more to lose—I must
Learn what my fate is. Just provide the way
To speak with her.

MARQUIS: You mean to show this letter   2390
To her? You really mean to do that?

CARLOS: Do
Not ask me. Now just find the way, the way.
I will speak with her!

MARQUIS: (*pointedly*)   Did you not tell me
You *loved* your mother?—Yet you mean to show
This letter to her?

                 (*Carlos looks at the ground in silence.*)
                     In your countenance,
Charles, I read something—wholly new to me—
And wholly alien until this moment—
You turn your eyes away from me? *Why* do
You turn your eyes away from me? Then it
Is true?—Did I hear rightly? Let me see—   2400
                (*Carlos gives him the letter. The
                Marquis tears it up.*)

CARLOS: What, are you mad?
                 (*with moderate irritation*)
                 I really will confess—
I set store by that letter.

MARQUIS: So it seemed.
That's why I tore it up.
(*The Marquis rests a piercing glance upon the Prince, who
looks at him dubiously. A long silence.*)
                 But tell me—What
Have desecrations of the royal bed
To do in any case with your—your love?
Was Philip dangerous to you? What link
Can possibly connect the husband's broken

Obligations with your bolder hopes?
Has he sinned, while you loved? O now I really
Begin to comprehend you. Up till now   2410
How poorly I have understood your love!
CARLOS: What, Roderick? What are you thinking?
MARQUIS: O,
  I sense what I must wean you from. Yes, once,
  Once all was very different. Then you were
  So rich, so warm, so rich! A universe
  Entire had space in your wide heart. All that
  Is over now and done, devoured by
  One passion, by a small self-interest.
  Your heart is dead within you. Not a tear
  Left for the Provinces' appalling fate,   2420
  Not even one tear left?—O Charles, how poor
  You have become, how beggar-poor, since you
  Love no one but yourself.
CARLOS:

  (*throws himself into an arm-chair.—After a pause, with barely
      suppressed tears*)
                          I know you have
  No more respect for me.
MARQUIS: Not so, Charles! No!
  I understand this agitation. It was
  An aberration of praiseworthy feelings.
  The Queen belonged to you, and by the Monarch
  Was stolen from you—and yet up till now
  You had your modest doubts about your rights.
  It might be Philip was deserving of her.   2430
  You hardly dared to pass a final judgment.
  That note decided you. With haughty joy you saw
  The fate of tyranny convicted of
  A theft. To be the injured party made you
  Exultant. For enduring wrongs delights
  Great souls. But there your fancy went awry,
  Your pride knew *satisfaction*—but your heart

Allowed itself to *hope*. You see, I knew
You had this time misunderstood yourself.   2440
CARLOS: *(touched)*
No, Roderick, you are quite wrong. I did
Not think so nobly, not by far, as you
Would like to make me think.
MARQUIS: Am I so little
Acquainted with your character? Look, Charles,
Whenever you do wrong, I always try
To single out that virtue among hundreds
To which I can trace back the error. But
Now that we understand each other better,
So be it! You shall see the Queen, you must
See her.—
CARLOS: *(falling upon his neck)*
                    O how I blush compared with you!   2450
MARQUIS: You have my word. Now leave the rest to me.
A wild, audacious, fortunate idea
Is rising now within my fancy—You
Shall hear it, Charles, from lips more beautiful.
I'll force my way to see the Queen. Perhaps
The outcome will be manifest tomorrow.
Until then, Charles, do not forget: "A notion
Born of the higher reason, urged by woes
Of human kind, ten thousand times defeated,
Must never be abandoned."—Do you hear?   2460
Remember Flanders!
CARLOS: Anything that *you*
And lofty virtue bid me, anything!
MARQUIS: *(walks to a window.)*
Our time is up. I hear your retinue.
                    (They embrace each other.)
Now vassal and Crown Prince again.
CARLOS: You're going
Right to the city now?
MARQUIS: At once.

CARLOS: One word yet!
  How easily it was forgotten!—News
  Most vital to you:—Letters to Brabant
  Are opened by the King. Be on your guard!
  Imperial couriers, I know, have secret
  Instructions—
MARQUIS: How did you learn that?
CARLOS: Don Raimond   2470
  Of Taxis is a friend of mine.
MARQUIS: *(after a silence)*   That yet!
  Then they will go around by Germany!   (2472)
           (They leave by different doors.)

ACT III

The King's bedchamber.
On the night table two lighted candles. In the background several pages on their knees, asleep. The King, with the upper part of his body half undressed, is standing in front of the table, one arm bent over the arm-chair, in a posture of meditation. In front of him lie a medallion and papers.

KING: That she was ardent-spirited—who can
  Deny it? *I* could never give her love,
  Yet—did she ever seem to feel the lack?
  Then it is proven, she is false.
    (*At this point he makes a movement that brings him to*
    himself. He looks up with surprise.)
                   Where was I?
  Is no one but the King awake here?—What?
  The candles all burned down? but not yet daylight?—
  I have been cheated of my slumber. Nature,
  Assume that it has been received. A King does not   2480
  Have time to make up for nights lost; I am
  Awake now and it shall be day.
    (*He extinguishes the candles and opens the curtains of one*
    window.—As he paces back and forth he notices the sleep-
    ing boys and stops for a time in silence before them; then
    he pulls the bell-cord.)
                   And are
  They sleeping in my antechamber too?
          (*Enter Count Lerma.*)

LERMA: (*startled at perceiving the King*)
   But is Your Majesty not well?
KING: There was
   A fire in the left pavilion. Did you
   Not hear the uproar?
LERMA: No, Your Majesty.
KING: No? How is that? Could I have only dreamed it?
   That could not come about by accident.
   Does not the Queen sleep in that wing?
LERMA: Why, yes,
   Your Majesty.
KING: The dream fills me with horror.   2490
   Let the guard henceforth be doubled there,
   You hear? as soon as evening comes—but quite,
   Quite secretly.—I do not want the Queen to—
   You probe me with your glances?
LERMA: I discern
   A burning eye that begs for slumber. May
   I venture to remind Your Majesty
   Of a most precious life, recalling also
   Whole nations that with pained surprise would read
   The traces of a wakeful night upon
   Such features—Only two brief morning hours   2500
   Of sleep—
KING: (*with troubled look*)
            Of sleep? In the Escurial
   I shall find sleep. Just so long as the King
   Is sleeping, he is cheated of his crown,
   The man is cheated of his wife's heart.—No!
   No! It is slander—Was it not a woman,
   A woman who came whispering that to me?
   Woman's name is slander. The transgression
   Remains unsure until a man confirms it.
            (*to the pages, who meanwhile have awakened*)
   Go call Duke Alba!
                  (*Exeunt pages.*)

DON CARLOS

Count, come nearer. Is

It true?

(He stops before the Count, scrutinizing.)

O for a pulse-throb's length to have   2510

Omniscience!—Is it true? I am deceived?

Swear it, am I? Is it true?

LERMA: My great,

My best of Kings—

KING: *(recoiling)* King! Nothing more than King,

And King again!—No better answer than

An empty, hollow echo I smite here

Upon this rock desiring water, water

For my hot fever thirst—He gives me nothing

But molten gold.

LERMA: What might be true, my King?

KING: Nothing. Nothing. Leave me.

        (The Count starts to leave; he calls him

           back again.)

              You are married?

You are a father?

LERMA: Yes, Your Majesty.   2520

KING: A married man, and yet you dare to watch

The night through at your master's side? Your hair

Is silver grey, and yet you do not blush

For trusting in your wife's integrity?

Go home. And you will come upon her in

Your son's incestuous embrace. Believe

Your King, and go.—You stand in consternation?

You look at me with meaning in your glance

Because, perhaps, I have grey hair myself?

Unhappy man, reflect upon the matter.   2530

Queens do not stain their virtue. You will be

A dead man if you doubt—

LERMA: *(heatedly)*   Who can do so?

In all the states my King possesses, who

Is insolent enough to breathe a poisoned

Suspicion of angelic purity?
So gravely to offend the best of Queens?—
KING: The best? So she is your best also? She
Has very ardent friends, I find, around me.
They must have cost her very dear—more than
I am aware she can afford to pay.   2540
You are dismissed now. Have the Duke sent in.
LERMA: I hear him in the anteroom—
                    (*on the point of leaving*)
KING: (*in a kindlier tone*)   Count, what
You previously observed was true. My head
Is burning from a wakeful night.—Forget
What I have said in waking dreams. You hear?
Forget it. I am still your gracious King.
    (*He gives him his hand to kiss. Lerma leaves and opens the
        door for the Duke of Alba.*)
ALBA: (*approaches the King with an uncertain look.*)
You send me this astonishing command—
At this extraordinary hour?
    (*He is startled as he looks more closely
        at the King.*)   And your
Appearance—
KING: (*has sat down and seized the medallion on the table. He
    looks at the Duke for a long time in silence.*)
                    So, then, it is really true?
I do not have a loyal servant?
ALBA: (*stops startled.*)   What?   2550
KING: I have been mortally offended—it
Is known, and no one warned me!
ALBA: (*with a look of amazement*) An offense
Which bears upon my King and which escaped
My eye?
KING: (*shows him the letter.*)
                You recognize this hand?
ALBA: It is
Don Carlos' hand—

KING: (*A pause, during which he observes the Duke sharply.*)
                    And still you do not guess?
You warned me on the score of his ambition?
But was it his ambition only I
Should tremble at?
ALBA: Ambition is a large—
Inclusive word where infinitely more
May be contained.
KING: And have you nothing special   2560
You might reveal to me?
ALBA: (*after a silence and glance of reservation*)
                    Your Majesty
Has placed the Empire in my watchful care.
I owe the Empire my most secret knowledge
And my discernment. But whatever else
I may suspect, or think, or know, belongs
To me alone. There are some consecrated
Possessions which the purchased slave, just like
The vassal, has the privilege of withholding
From all the kings on earth.—Not everything
That stands quite clear before *my* soul, is ripe   2570
Enough to tell my King. But if he wishes
Satisfaction, I must beg him not
To ask as master.
KING: (*gives him the letters.*)
                    Read.
ALBA: (*reads and turns in horror to the King.*)
                    Who was
Insane enough to lay this wretched paper
In my King's hands?
KING: What? Then you know to whom
The contents are addressed?—The signature,
I know, has been omitted from the paper.
ALBA: (*recoiling, startled*)
I spoke too fast.
KING: You know?

ALBA: *(after some reflection)*   The word is out.
My Lord commands—I may retreat no longer—
Hence I will not deny—I know the person.   2580
KING: *(rising with a terrifying movement)*
O help me to invent new kinds of death,
You fearful god of vengeance!—So apparent
Is this collusion, so world-wide, so clear,
That people, spared the effort of a search,
Divine it at first glance—This is too much!
And I was not aware of it! Not that!
And so I am the last to find it out!
The last in all my kingdom—
ALBA: Yes, most gracious Monarch,
I will acknowledge myself guilty. I
Blush for my coward cleverness that bade me   2590
Be silent where the honor of my King,
As well as truth and justice, challenged me
Loudly enough to speak.—But inasmuch
As everyone is silent—inasmuch
As beauty's spell holds all men's tongues enchanted,
I shall make bold to speak; although I know
A son's insinuating protestations
And the seductive blandishments and tears
And lamentations of a wife will—
KING: *(suddenly and vehemently)*   Rise.
You have my royal word—I bid you rise   2600
And speak out unafraid.
ALBA: *(rising)*   Your Majesty
May still perhaps recall that incident
Down in the garden at Aranjuez.
You found the Queen abandoned by her ladies—
With disconcerted looks—alone amid
A distant arbor.
KING: Ha! What is it I
Am now to hear? Continue!
ALBA: The Marquise

Of Mondecar was banished from the realm
Because she had the magnanimity
To sacrifice herself to save her Queen.—   2610
We now have information—The Marquise
Had done no more than she had been commanded.—
The Prince had been there.
KING: *(with frightful passion)*   Been there! Then despite—
ALBA: The footprints of a man upon the sand
That led from the left entrance of that arbor
And vanished towards a grotto, where still lay
A handkerchief which the Infánt had missed,
Aroused suspicion right away. A gardner
Had met the Prince there, and that was the same
Time, calculated almost to the minute,   2620
At which Your Majesty made your appearance
Amid the arbor.
KING: *(coming out of a sombre meditation)*
                        And she wept when I
Gave evidence of my surprise. She made
Me blush in sight of all my courtiers!
And blush before myself.—By God! I stood
There like a convict sentenced by her virtue—
                    *(A long and profound silence. He sits
                    down and covers his face.)*
Ah yes, Duke Alba—you are right.—This could
Lead me to something horrible.—Leave me
Alone a moment.
ALBA: Even this, my King,
Does not decide conclusively—
KING: *(seizing the papers)*   Nor this?   2630
And this? And this again? And this loud chord
Of utterly condemnatory proofs?
O it is clearer than the light—What I
Had long known in advance—The mischief started
There in Madrid when for the first time I
Received her from your hands—I see her yet,

Pale as a ghost and dwelling with that look
Of horror at the sight of my grey hair.
It started then, her cheating game.

ALBA: The Prince
Had lost a bride in his young mother. They   2640
Had entertained desires within their hearts
And understood each other's ardent feelings,
Which her new state prohibited. The fear
Had been already overcome, the fear
Which usually attends a first avowal,
And thus temptation spoke more recklessly
In scenes in all propriety recalled.
Linked in the harmony of age and spirit,
Galled by the same compulsion, they responded
With all the more resolve to passion's surge.   2650
Politics forestalled their inclinations;
Is it conceivable, my Monarch, she
Would have acknowledged that state council's power?
That she subdued her sensuality
To test the council's choice with closer care?
She was prepared for love, and she received—
A diadem.

KING: (with hurt bitterness)
                You make distinctions very—
Very shrewdly, Duke.—I marvel at
Your eloquence. I thank you.
                (rising; coldly and proudly)
                You are right:
The Queen has gravely erred in her concealment   2660
From me of letters of such tenor—and
In keeping the Infante's culpable
Appearance in the garden secret from me.
False generosity caused her grave error.
I shall know how to punish her.
                (He pulls the bell-cord.)
                Who else

Is in the anteroom?—Duke Alba,
I have no further need of you. Withdraw.

ALBA: Can I have caused Your Majesty displeasure
A second time through zeal of mine?

KING: (*to a page who comes in*)   Have them
Admit Domingo.

                    (*Exit the page.*)
               I forgive you for   2670
The fact that for almost two minutes' time
You have inspired in *me* fear of a crime
Which can conceivably befall to *you*.
                  (*Alba withdraws.*)
  (*The King paces up and down a few times to collect him-
    self. Domingo enters a few minutes after the Duke, and
    approaches the King whom he observes for a time in
    solemn silence.*)

DOMINGO: How happily surprised I am to see
Your Majesty so calm and so composed—

KING: You are surprised—

DOMINGO: Thank Providence my fear
Was quite unfounded after all! I may
Then hope that much the more.

KING: Your fear? What was
There to be feared?

DOMINGO: Your Majesty, I may not
Conceal the fact that I already know   2680
About a secret—

KING: (*darkly*)   When did I express
The wish to share it with you? Who has thus
Anticipated me without my asking?
Upon my honor, that was rash!

DOMINGO: My Monarch,
The place and the occasion where I learned
Of it, the seal beneath which I learned of it,
These will at least absolve me of this guilt.
It was confided to me in confession—

Confided as a sin which weighs upon
The tender conscience of the penitent   2690
And sues to Heaven for remission now.
Too late the Princess rues a deed from which
She has good reason to surmise the dreadful
Consequences for her Queen.

KING: Indeed?
That gentle heart—You have divined quite rightly
The reason why I had you summoned. You
Must lead me out of this dark labyrinth
Into which blind zealousness has plunged me.
From you I look for truth. Speak openly
With me. What am I to believe, or think?   2700
I call upon your office for the truth.

DOMINGO: Sire, even if the mildness of my office
Did not enjoin sweet leniency upon me,
I still would urge upon Your Majesty,
And urge it for your own tranquillity,
To call a halt with what you have discovered—
Renounce forever probing of a secret
Which never can proceed to happiness.
What is now known can still admit forgiveness.
Let the King speak but one word only—and   2710
The Queen has never erred. The Monarch's will
Makes virtue just as it makes happiness—
And only my King's ever even calm
Can mightily refute the idle rumors
Which slander has allowed itself.

KING: What? Rumors?
About me and among my people?

DOMINGO: Lies!
Damnable, accursed lies, I swear!
Yet all the same there are occasions when
What people think, be it however groundless,
Becomes quite as significant as truth.   2720

KING: By God! This would be just the point—

DOMINGO: A good

Name is the precious, sole possession which
A Queen must vie for with the burgher's wife—

KING: For which, however, I should hope there is
No need to tremble for in this case.

               (*He rests an uncertain glance upon*
                   Domingo. After a silence.)

                            Chaplain,

I am to hear more evil from you yet.
Do not postpone it. I have long since read it
In that misfortune-bringing face of yours.
Out with it! Be it what it may! Let me
Not quiver any longer on this rack.   2730
What do the people think?

DOMINGO: Again, Sire, people
Can err—and err they surely do. What they
Assert must not distress the King.—However,
The fact that they have gone so far already
As to assert this sort of—

KING: What? Must I
Beg you so long for one small drop of poison?

DOMINGO: The memories of people still go back to
That month which brought Your Royal Majesty
So close to death—and thirty weeks thereafter
They read the news about the fortunate   2740
Delivery—

         (*The King rises and pulls the bell cord.*
         Enter the Duke of Alba. Domingo is astonished.)
           Sire, I am amazed!

KING: (*walking toward the Duke of Alba*)   Toledo!
You are a man. Protect me from this priest.

DOMINGO:

    (*He and the Duke of Alba exchange looks of embarrassment.*
      After a pause)

If we could possibly have known beforehand
That this report might be avenged upon

    Its bringer—

KING: Bastard, do you say? I was,
    You say, but scarcely risen from the dead
    When she perceived her motherhood?—That was,
    If I am not in error, just the time
    When you were praising Holy Dominic
    In all the churches for the lofty miracle   2750
    That he had wrought upon me?—What was then
    A miracle is one no longer now?
    In that case you were lying then, or else
    You have lied here today. In what would you
    Have me believe? O, I see through you. If
    Your plot had been ripe then,—yes, then the Saint
    Would have been cheated of his glory.

ALBA: Plot!

KING: You should
    Concur now in the same opinion, with
    This unexampled harmony, and yet
    Not have a previous understanding? Is   2760
    That what you would persuade me of? Me? I
    Am not supposed to notice how intently
    And greedily you fell upon your prey?
    Or with what lust you feasted on my grief
    And on the agitation of my anger?
    No more am I supposed to see how full
    Of zeal the Duke there burns to snatch the favor
    Which was accorded to my son? Or how
    This pious man would gladly implement
    His petty grudge with my wrath's giant arm?   2770
    I am the bow, is that what you imagine,
    The bow that anyone may bend at will?—
    I also have my own will yet—and if
    I am to have some doubts, let me at least
    Begin with you.

ALBA: Our loyalty did not
    Expect this application.

KING: Loyalty!
  Loyalty warns of impending crimes,
  Vindictiveness speaks of committed ones.
  Let me hear! What would I gain by your
  Officiousness?—If what you claim is true,   2780
  What have I left but the wound of divorce?
  The sorry triumph of revenge?—But no,
  You merely fear, you give me fluctuating
  Surmises—On the brink of an inferno
  You leave me standing and take flight.

DOMINGO: Are other
  Proofs possible, when here the eye itself
  Declines to be convinced?

KING: *(after a long pause, turning earnestly and solemnly to*
   Domingo)
                              I shall convoke
  The grandees of my kingdom and myself
  Shall sit in judgment. Come before them all
  At that assembly—if you have the courage—   2790
  And name her an adulteress!—Then she
  Shall die the death—without appeal—both she
  And the Infánt shall die—but—mark you well!
  If she can justify herself—then you shall die!
  Now will you offer Truth that sacrifice?
  Make up your minds. You will not? You are silent?
  You will not?—This is liars' zealousness.

ALBA: *(who has stood silently apart, coldly and quietly)*
  I will.

KING: *(turns in astonishment and looks at the Duke fixedly*
   for a time)
       Ah, that is bold!—But it occurs
  To me that you have risked your life for things
  Far less significant in bitter battles—   2800
  And risked it with a dicing player's rashness
  For the non-entity of fame.—And what
  Is life to you?—The King's blood royal I

Will not abandon to a madman who
Can hope for no more than to yield his petty
Existence up sublimely.—I reject
Your sacrifice. Go—go, and wait out in
The audience chamber for my further orders.
(Exeunt both.)

KING: (alone)
Good Providence, give me a human being—
Much hast thou given me. But send me now   2810
A human being. Thou—thou art alone,
For thy eyes penetrate to hidden things—
I beg thee for a friend, for I am not,
Like thee, omniscient. The assistants whom
Thou hast appointed for me—what they are
Thou knowest. As their merits are, so have
I valued them. Their tame and little vices,
Checked by the reins, have served my purposes,
Just as thy tempests purify the world.
But I need truth—and digging clear its quiet   2820
Fountain in the murky sludge of error
Is not the lot of kings. O vouchsafe me
That rare man with a pure and open heart,
With bright clear spirit and impartial eyes,
Who can help me to find it.—I shake forth
The lots; O let me find amid the thousands
That flit about the sun of Majesty
That single, unique man.
(He opens a casket and takes out a writing
tablet. After leafing through it for a time)
Mere names—names only
Are here recorded, with not even mention
Made of the service which they have to thank   2830
For their place in this register.—And what
Is sooner out of mind than gratitude?
Yet here upon this other tablet I
Read every fault precisely margin-noted.

How so? That is not good. Can thought of vengeance
Need this reminder yet?
                    (*He reads on.*)
                    Count Egmont? Why
Should he be here?—His triumph at Saint Quentin
Was long since forfeit. I throw him to the dead.
                    (*He erases this name and writes it on
                    the other tablet. After reading further*)
Marquis of Posa?—Posa?—Posa? Why,
I hardly can remember such a person!   2840
And underlined with double bar—proof that
I had him designated for great ends.
And, was it possible, this man has kept
His distance from my presence until now?
Avoided the eye of his royal debtor?
By God! in the whole circuit of my states
The only man who has no need of me!
If he had greed for goods or honors, he
Would long since have appeared before my throne.
Shall I risk this odd character? One who   2850
Can do without me will have truth for me.

                    (*Exit.*)

SCENE 2

The audience chamber.
*Don Carlos in conversation with the Prince of Parma. The
Dukes of Alba, Feria, and Medina Sidonia. Count of Lerma
and still other grandees with papers in their hands. All are
expecting the King.*

MEDINA SIDONIA: (*obviously avoided by all present, turns to
        the Duke of Alba, who is pacing back and forth alone and
        preoccupied*)

You have had converse with our master, Duke—
In what mood did you find him?

ALBA: Very bad
For you and for your tidings.

MEDINA SIDONIA: In the fire
Of English guns I found it easier
Than on this pavement here.

    (Carlos, who has been gazing at him with quiet sympathy,
    now approaches him and presses his hand.)

                              My warmest thanks,
Prince, for this generous-hearted tear. You see
How everyone avoids me. Now my downfall
Is settled.

CARLOS: Hope, friend, for the best both from
My father's mercy and your innocence.   2860

MEDINA SIDONIA: I lost a fleet for him the like of which had not
Appeared before upon the sea.—What is
A head like mine compared to seventy
Destroyed and sunken galleons?—But, Prince—
Five sons, as full of hope as you—that breaks
My heart—

    (Enter the King in full attire. All remove their hats and step
    back on both sides as they form a semicircle about him.
    Silence.)

KING: *(glancing cursorily over the entire circle)*
               Be covered!

    (Don Carlos and the Prince of Parma approach first and kiss
    the King's hand. He turns with a certain friendliness to
    the latter without taking any notice of his son.)

                  From your mother, Nephew,
Comes the inquiry how well people are
Pleased with you in Madrid.

PARMA: Let her not ask
Before the outcome of my maiden battle.

KING: On that score set your mind at rest. Your turn   2870
Will come some day when these supports give way.

(to the Duke of Feria)

What do you bring me?

FERIA: *(genuflecting before the King)*
                                  The Commander of
The Order of Calatrava died this morning.
His knight's cross is herewith returned.

KING: *(takes the order and looks around the entire circle.)*
                                  Who will
Be worthiest to wear it after him?
　　*(He beckons Alba to him, who genuflects before him, and
　　hangs the order around his neck.)*
Duke, you are my first General—Be no *more*
And you will never find my favor lacking.
　　　　　*(He becomes aware of the Duke of
　　　　　　　　Medina Sidonia.)*
Aha! my admiral!

MEDINA SIDONIA: *(approaches falteringly and kneels before the
　　King with head bowed.)*
                          This, my great King,
Is all I bring back of the Spanish youth
And the Armada.

KING: *(after a long silence)*   2880
                          God is over me—
I sent it to contend with human beings,
Not to contend with rocks and tempest—You
Are welcome in Madrid.
　　　　　(He extends him his hand to kiss.)
                          And thanks for having
Preserved for me a worthy servant in
Yourself!—I here acknowledge him before
These my grandees, and would have him acknowledged.
　　*(He signs him to rise and be covered—then he turns towards
　　the others.)*
What further is there?
　　　　　(to Don Carlos and the Prince of Parma)
                          I thank you, my Princes.

*(The latter withdraw. The remaining grandees approach
and, kneeling, present their papers to the King. He scans
them quickly and hands them to the Duke of Alba.)*
Put all those in my study.—Have I finished now?
                    (No one answers.)
How does it happen that among all my
Grandees a Marquis Posa never comes?   2890
I am aware this Marquis Posa has
Served me with glory. Is he dead perhaps?
Why does he not appear?
LERMA: The cavalier
Has only recently arrived from travels
Which he has undertaken throughout Europe.
He has but just come to Madrid and only
Waits for the day of public audiences
To throw himself before his Sovereign's feet.
ALBA: Marquis of Posa?—Right! That is the gallant
Youth, Your Majesty, and Knight of Malta   2900
About whom fame reports the dashing deed.
When at the bidding of the Order's Master
The knights took up position on their island,
Which Soliman laid under siege, this youth
Of eighteen vanished suddenly out of
Alcala's upper school. Unsummoned he
Stood there in front of La Valette. "My cross
Was bought," said he, "and now I want to earn it."
He was one of those forty knights who held
Saint Elmo Fort in three successive stormings   2910
By broad noonday against Piali and
Ulucciali, Mustafa and Hassem.
When finally the citadel was scaled
And round about it all the knights were slain,
He threw himself into the sea and came
The sole survivor back to La Valette.
The enemy two months thereafter left
The island, and the knight returned to school

To finish studies that he had begun.

FERIA: It was this Marquis Posa also who   2920
Discovered subsequently the appalling
Conspiracy in Catalonia
And merely by his skill alone preserved
That most important province for the crown.

KING: I am amazed—What sort of man is this
Who did all *that,* and of the three I ask,
Not one of you is jealous of him?—Surely
This man has most unusual character
Or none at all.—Sheer rarity demands
I should make his acquaintance.
> *(to the Duke of Alba)*
> After Mass   2930

Bring him to me within my study.
> *(Exit the Duke.)*
> *(The King calls Feria.)*
> And you

Shall sit in my place in the Privy Council.
> *(Exit.)*

FERIA: The King is well disposed today.

MEDINA SIDONIA: Say rather
He is a god!—He has been one to me.

FERIA: How very well you merit your good fortune!
I sympathize most warmly, Admiral.

FIRST GRANDEE: And I.

SECOND GRANDEE: And I, indeed.

THIRD GRANDEE: My heart leaped up.
Such a deserving General!

FIRST GRANDEE: The King
Did not show mercy to you—only justice.

LERMA: *(to Medina Sidonia on the way out)*
How two words suddenly have made you rich!   2940

(Exeunt omnes.)

SCENE 3

The King's study.
Marquis of Posa and the Duke of Alba.

MARQUIS: *(entering)*
    He wants to see me? Me?—That cannot be.
    You are mistaken in the name.—What does
    He want of me?
ALBA: He wants to meet you.
MARQUIS: Merely
    From curiosity?—In that case, what
    A pity for the wasted moment.—Life
    Is over so astonishingly fast.
ALBA: I give
    You over to your lucky star. The King
    Is in your hands. Make use, as well as you
    Are able, of this moment, and blame no one,
    Blame no one but yourself if it is lost.   2950
                  (He withdraws.)
MARQUIS: *(alone)*
    Well spoken, Duke. The moment must be used,
    The moment which presents itself *once* only.
    In very truth this courtier gives me good
    Advice—and even if it is not good
    In his sense, all the same it is in mine.
             (after some pacing back and forth)
    But how did I get here?—Could it be only
    The whim of a capricious circumstance
    Which now reflects my image in *these* mirrors?
    Which from a million others seized on me,
    The most unlikely of them all, and brought   2960
    To life the recollection of the King?
    A mere coincidence? Perhaps more too—
    What is coincidence but the rough stone

That takes on life beneath the sculptor's hand?
Coincidences are from Providence—
And man must shape them to a purpose.—What
The King wants of me is no matter!—I
Know what I must do with the King.—And even
If it were no more than a spark of truth
But boldly flung into the despot's soul,—   2970
How awesome is the hand of Providence!
Thus what seemed so capricious first may be
Intentional and fraught with meaning. So,
Or not so—I shall act in this belief.

> (*He takes several turns through the room and finally stops
> in tranquil contemplation of a painting. The King be-
> comes visible in the adjoining room, where he is issuing
> some orders. Then he enters, stands quietly at the door
> and for a time observes the Marquis without being
> noticed by him.*
>
> *The latter, as soon as he is aware of him, walks toward the
> King, genuflects before him, rises, and remains standing in
> front of him without any sign of perturbation.*)

KING: (*observes him with a look of amazement.*)
You have met me before, then?
MARQUIS: No.
KING: You made
My Crown indebted to you. Why have you
Fought shy of seeking thanks from me? Within
My memory are crowded many people.
But One alone knows everything. It was
Your place to seek out the eye of your King.   2980
Why did you not do so?
MARQUIS: It was a couple
Of days ago that I returned, Sire, to
Your kingdom.
KING: I am not inclined to stand
Indebted to the persons in my service.
Entreat some favor from me.

MARQUIS: I enjoy the laws.
KING: The murderer also has that right.
MARQUIS: How much
   More the good citizen!—I am content, Sire.
KING: (*to himself*)
   By God! Much self-reliance and bold spirit.
   That was to be expected, though.—I want
   A Spaniard to be proud. I even like   2990
   It when the cup runs over.—I hear that
   You have resigned my service?
MARQUIS: I withdrew
   To make room for a better man.
KING: That grieves me.
   If heads the like of this make holiday,
   How great the loss is for my state.—Perhaps
   You are afraid that you will miss the sphere
   Which would be worthy of your mind.
MARQUIS: Oh, no!
   I feel quite certain the experienced knower
   Of human souls—his matter—will have read
   With practiced skill and at first glance what worth   3000
   I can or cannot be to him. I feel
   With humble gratitude the favor which
   Your Royal Majesty is heaping on me
   By the expression of this proud opinion.
   However—
                    (*He checks himself.*)
KING: You deliberate?
MARQUIS: I am—
   I must confess, Sire, not prepared just now
   To clothe in words that fit one of your subjects
   The things that I thought as world-citizen.—
   For at the time, Sire, when I had forever
   Cut my connections with the Crown, I felt   3010
   Myself released from all necessity
   Of giving reasons to it for that step.

KING: Your reasons are that weak? Are you afraid
   To venture them?
MARQUIS: If I took time, Sire, to
   Exhaust the list—my lifetime would be needed.
   But I will jeopardize the truth if you
   Refuse that favor. For the choice is left me
   Of either your contempt or your displeasure—
   If this decision must be made by me,
   Then I prefer to go out of your sight   3020
   A criminal but not a fool.
KING: (*with expectant look*)   Well, then?
MARQUIS: —I cannot be the server of a Prince.
         (*The King looks at him in astonishment.*)
   I will not cheat the buyer, Sire.—If you
   Do me the honor of appointing me,
   Then you want only the deed preassigned.
   You want my arm alone and valor in
   The field, my mind in council. Not my deeds,
   But their approval found before the throne,
   Shall be the goal of action. But for me
   Right conduct has a value of its own.   3030
   The happiness the Monarch would plant by
   My hands, if I myself created it,
   Then duty would be joy and my own choice.
   But is that your opinion too? Can you
   Bear strange creators in your own creation?
   Must I descend to be a chisel merely
   When I might be the sculptor?—My love is
   To all mankind; in monarchies I may
   Love no one but myself.
KING: This ardor is
   Praiseworthy. You wish to establish Good.   3040
   How you establish it is no great matter
   To patriots or men of wisdom. Choose
   Yourself a post within my range of kingdoms
   Which will empower you to give scope to

This noble impulse.
MARQUIS: I have found none.
KING: What?
MARQUIS: That which Your Majesty would spread abroad
   By my hand—Is that human happiness?—
   Is it the kind of happiness that my
   Pure love grants human beings?—Majesty
   Would tremble at that happiness.—Oh no!   3050
   Crown policy created a new kind—
   That *it* is rich enough to spread abroad,
   And in the human heart new impulses
   That can be gratified by that new kind.
   Upon its coins it has Truth struck, *that* truth
   Which it can tolerate. All other stamps
   Are thrown away that are not like that *one*.
   But what is to the Crown's advantage—will
   It be enough for me? Shall my love for
   My brother be lent to encroachment on   3060
   My brother? Do I know that he is happy
   Before he is allowed to think? Do not
   Choose me, Sire, to spread happiness that you
   Have stamped. I must refuse to pass those stamps.—
   I cannot be the server of a Prince.
KING: (*rather suddenly*)
   You are a Protestant.
MARQUIS: (*after some reflection*)   Your faith, Sire, is
   Mine also.

                    (*after a pause*)
   I have been misunderstood.
   That was just what I feared. You see the veil
   Withdrawn by my hand from the mysteries
   Of majesty. Who will give you assurance   3070
   That what has ceased to terrify me will
   Still be accounted holy by me? I
   Am dangerous because I have done thinking
   About myself.—But I am not, my King.

My wishes molder here.
                    (*his hand upon his heart*)
                    The foolish craze
For revolution, which but makes more heavy
The weight of chains it cannot wholly break,
Will never fire *my* blood. The century
Is not yet ripe for my ideal. I
Live as a citizen of those to come.   3080
Can a mere picture trouble your repose?—
Your breath effaces it.

KING: Am I the first
To know this side of you?

MARQUIS: This side of—Yes!

KING: (*rises, walks a few paces, and stops opposite the Marquis.
    To himself*)
At least this tone is novel! Flattery
Exhausts itself. To imitate the others
Degrades a man of talent.—Shall the test
Be made once of the opposite? Why not?
Surprises make for pleasure.—Good, then. If
You understand the thing so well, I shall
Arrange for a new Crown administration—   3090
For your strong mind—

MARQUIS: I notice, Sire, how small,
How low you rate the dignity of man,
And even in the free man's speech see only
The cunning of the flatterer, and I
Believe I know who warrants your conception.
Human beings forced you to it; *they*
Of their free will sold their nobility,
Of their free will reduced themselves to this
Base level. Terrified they flee before
The ghost of their own inner greatness, take   3100
A pleasure in their poverty, adorn
Their chains with wisdom born of cowardice,
And call it virtue when they wear them with

Decorum. Thus you overcame the world.
So it was given you by your great father.
In this pathetic mutilated form
How could you—honor human beings?

KING: In

Your words I find some truth.

MARQUIS: Alas, however!
When from the hand of the Creator you
Transformed these men into your handiwork   3110
And to this newly molded creature set
Yourself up as a god—you overlooked
One item: you yourself remained a man—
A man from the Creator's hand. *You* went
On suffering as a mortal, and desiring;
Now *you* need sympathy—and with a god
Men can only tremble—sacrifice—
And pray! Regrettable exchange! Unhappy
Distortion of the way of Nature!—Since
You lowered man to be your instrument   3120
Who will share harmony with you?

KING: (By God,
He strikes into my soul!)

MARQUIS: This sacrifice,
However, has no meaning for you. For
You are unique—a class unto yourself—
And at this price you are a god.—How dreadful
If it were *not* so—if at this price, at
Cost of the trampled happiness of millions,
They had gained nothing! if the freedom which
You have annihilated were the only
Thing that could bring your wishes to fruition?—   3130
I beg you to dismiss me, Sire. My subject
Sweeps me away. My heart is full—the charm
Too great of standing with the only man
To whom I would like to reveal it.

(*The Count of Lerma enters and speaks a few words softly*

*to the King. The latter signs him to withdraw, and re-
mains sitting in his former position.*)

KING: (*to the Marquis after Lerma has gone out*)
                                    Go

On speaking.

MARQUIS: (*after some silence*)
                        Sire, I feel—the entire merit—

KING: Conclude! You had still more to say to me.

MARQUIS: Sire, I have just come from Brabant and Flanders—
So many flourishing, rich provinces!
A great and sturdy people—and a good
People also—Father of that people!   3140
To be that, I thought, must be god-like!—Then
I came upon charred bones of human beings—
    (*Here he falls silent. His eyes rest upon the King, who tries
    to meet this glance but looks at the ground startled and
    confused.*)
But you are right. *You* had to. That you *can*
Do what you realized you had to, filled
Me with a horrified astonishment.
A pity that the victim drowned in his
Own blood cannot intone a hymn of praise to
The spirit of the executioner!
Or that mere human beings—and not creatures
Of higher kind—write history!—But gentler   3150
Ages will supplant the times of Philip;
They will bring milder wisdom; welfare of
The citizen will walk with Princes' greatness
In harmony, the thrifty state will cherish
Its children, and Necessity be human.

KING: When do you think these human centuries
Would come about, had I not trembled at
The curse that plagues the present one? Look
About you in this Spain of mine. The welfare
Of citizens blooms here in cloudless peace;   3160
And *this peace* I grant to the Flemish people.

MARQUIS: (*quickly*)
 The peace of cemeteries! And you hope
 To finish what you have begun? You hope
 To halt the transformation of matured
 Christendom, the universal springtime
 That makes the world's form young again?—You want—
 Alone in all of Europe—to oppose
 The wheel of universal destiny
 Now rolling beyond check in full career,
 And thrust your human arm between its spokes?   3170
 You will not! Thousands have already fled
 From your lands poor but happy. And the subjects
 That you have lost for the Faith's sake were your
 Most noble ones. With mother's arms wide opened
 Elizabeth receives the fugitives,
 And with the skills of our lands Britain blooms
 Luxuriantly. Granada lies a waste
 For want of industry of "the new Christians",
 And Europe gloats to see its enemy
 Bleeding to death from self-inflicted wounds.   3180
   (*The King is moved; the Marquis perceives
    it and comes several steps closer.*)
 You want to plant for all eternity,
 And you sow death? No work done thus by force
 Will last beyond the will of its creator.
 You have built for ingratitude—for naught
 You have fought your hard fight with Nature, and
 For naught expended your great royal life
 In sacrifice for projects of destruction.
 Man is a greater thing than you have thought him.
 And he will burst the bonds of lengthy slumber
 And will demand his consecrated rights.   3190
 Your name with Nero's and Busiris' he
 Will vilify, and—that is painful to me,
 For you were good.
KING: Who gave you such assurance

That this is so?

MARQUIS: *(with ardor)*   Yes, by Almighty God!
Yes—Yes—and I repeat it. Give us back
What you have taken from us. Generously,
As a strong man, let human happiness
Stream forth out of your horn of plenty.—Minds
In your world-edifice are ripening.
Give us back what you have taken from us.   3200
Become a King among a million kings.
                    (*He approaches him boldly while
                    directing firm and fiery glances at him.*)
O, if upon my lips might hover that
Persuasiveness of all the thousands who
Share the concern in this momentous hour,
To fan into a flame the ray that I
Perceive now in your eyes! Abjure all this
Unnatural deification which
Annihilates us, and become our pattern
Of the eternal truth. O never—never
Did mortal man possess so much, to use   3210
In such a god-like fashion. All the kings
Of Europe venerate the Spanish name.
Walk at the head of all the kings of Europe.
A single pen-stroke will suffice: the world
Will be created new. O give us freedom
Of thought—
                    (*throwing himself at his feet*)
KING: (*taken by surprise, with face averted and then again
    fixed on the Marquis*)
                    Fantastic visionary! But—
Stand up—I—
MARQUIS: Cast your eye about you in
The splendor of His Nature! It is founded
On freedom—and how rich it is by virtue
Of freedom! He, the great Creator, casts   3220
The worm into a drop of dew and lets

Free will take its delight amid the very
Death spaces of corruption—Your creation,
How cramped and poor! The rustling of a leaf
Strikes terror in the lord of Christendom—
You must fear every virtue. *He*—lest Freedom's
Delightful presence be disturbed—He sooner
Allows the entire ghastly host of Evil
To rage throughout His universe—Of Him,
The Maker, one is not aware; discreetly   3230
He veils Himself in His eternal laws.
The free-thinker sees *these,* but not *Him.* Why have
A God? says he; the world is self-sufficient.
No Christian's piety has ever praised
Him more than that free-thinker's blasphemy.
KING: And would you undertake to imitate
This pattern of sublimity among
The mortal creatures in my kingdoms?
MARQUIS: You,
You can do so. Who else can? Consecrate
The ruling power to the welfare of   3240
The peoples who—so long—have served but to
Promote the greatness of the throne. Restore
Mankind its lost nobility. And let
The subject be once more what he once was,
The purpose of the Crown,—and let no duty
Bind him but his brothers' equally
Sacred rights. Once man, returned unto
Himself, wakes to awareness of his worth—
And Freedom's proud and lofty virtues thrive—
Then, Sire, when you have made your own realm into   3250
The happiest in the world—then it will be
Your obligation to subject the world.
KING: (*after a great silence*)
I have let you speak to the end—The world,
I understand, is not depicted in
Your mind as in the minds of others—nor

Will I subject you to an alien standard.
I am the first to whom you have revealed your inmost
Thoughts. That much I believe, because I know it.
And for the sake of your forbearance in
Maintaining silence until now on these   3260
Opinions held with such great ardor—for
This prudence and discretion's sake, young man,
I will forget that I have learned of them
And how I learned of them. Arise. I shall
Refute the youth who overstepped the limits,
As one of riper years but not as King.
I shall, because I wish to.—Even poison
Itself, I find, may be transmuted in
High natures into something better.—But
Avoid my Inquisition. It would pain   3270
Me—

MARQUIS: Would it? Really?

KING: (*lost in gazing at him*) Such a human being
I never saw before.—No! No, Marquis!
You have read too much into me. I wish
To be no Nero. That I do not want—
Not in respect to you. Not all
Of happiness shall wither under me.
Beneath my eyes you may yourself continue
To be a human being.

MARQUIS: (*quickly*)   Sire, what of
My fellow-citizens? O, I was not
Concerned with me, I did not wish to plead   3280
My cause. What of your subjects, Sire?—

KING: And if
You know so well how centuries to come
Will judge me, let them learn by you how I
Have acted with a human being when
I found one.

MARQUIS: O let the most just of kings

Be not all of a sudden the most unjust—
In your own Flanders there are thousands better
Than I. And *you* alone—may I assume
The liberty, great King, to speak it frankly?—
Beneath this milder picture *you* are seeing   3290
Freedom now perhaps for the first time.
KING: (*with mitigated seriousness*)
No more, young man, upon this subject.—I
Know you will think quite differently when you
Know human beings as I know them.—Yet
I should not like to have this be the last
Time I see you. What shall I do to win you?
MARQUIS: Let me be as I am. What good would I
Be to you, Sire, were you to bribe me?
KING: This
Pride I cannot endure. You are from this
Day forward in my service—No objections!   3300
I will have it so.

                    (*after a pause*)
                    And yet—What was it
I wanted? Was it not truth that I wanted?
I find here something more besides.—You have
Now found me out upon my throne, Marquis;
But in my private life?
                    (*as the Marquis seems to deliberate*)
                    I understand you.
But—Were I not the most unfortunate
Of fathers, can I not be happy as
A husband?
MARQUIS: If a son replete with promise,
If the possession of the loveliest
Of spouses, gives a mortal man the right   3310
To be so called, Sire, then you are on both
Counts the most fortunate of men.
KING: (*with a dark look*)   No, that

I am not! And I never felt more deeply
Than now that I am not—
                    (*dwelling with a gaze of sadness upon*
                            the Marquis)
MARQUIS: The Prince's thoughts
Are good and noble. I have never found
Him otherwise.
KING: But I have.—No crown can
Make up for me what he has taken from me—
A Queen so virtuous!
MARQUIS: Sire, who would dare
Do such a thing?
KING: The world! Its blasphemies!
And I myself!—Here lie the proofs that damn her   3320
Incontrovertibly; and there are others
Available besides, that make me fear
The utmost—But, Marquis, I find it hard,
Hard to believe *one thing*. Who is it that
Accuses her?—If *she*—she ever could
Have brought such deep dishonor on herself,
O how much more may I permit myself
To think an Eboli is slandering?
Does not the Priest hate both my son and her?
And am I not aware that Alba broods   3330
Revenge? My wife is worth more than them all.
MARQUIS: Sire, something else still lives in your wife's soul
That is exalted over all appearance
And over every blasphemy—its name
Is womanly virtue.
KING: Yes! So I say too.
To sink so low as they accuse the Queen
Of sinking, takes a lot. So easily
As they would like to make me think, fine bonds
Of honor do not break. You know mankind,
Marquis. I long have felt the need of such   3340
A man as you. You are both good and cheerful

And yet you also know mankind—Therefore
I choose you—
MARQUIS: *(surprised and startled)*
                    Me, Sire?
KING: You have stood before
Your lord and have asked nothing for yourself—
Nothing. That is new to me.—You will
Be just. Your glance will not be led astray
By passion—Make your way to my son's favor,
And sound the Queen's heart out. I will send you
Full authorization to speak with them both
In private. Leave me now.
                    (He pulls the bell cord.)
MARQUIS: Can I do so   3350
With *one* hope realized? If so, this day
Will be the finest of my life.
KING: *(gives him his hand to kiss.)* It is
No lost one in *my* life.
                    (The Marquis rises and leaves.)
                    (Enter Count Lerma.)
                    The cavalier
Will henceforth be admitted unannounced.   (3354)

ACT IV

A room in the Queen's apartments.
The Queen, Duchess Olivarez, the Princess of Eboli, the Count-
ess Fuentes, and other ladies.

QUEEN: *(to the chief stewardess, as she rises)*
    The key, then, was not to be found?—Then I
    Shall have to have the casket broken open,
    And that directly—
        (as she becomes aware of the Princess
          of Eboli, who approaches her and kisses
          her hand)
                    Welcome, my dear Princess.
    I am delighted to find you restored
    To health—Still, to be sure, quite pale—
FUENTES: *(somewhat maliciously)*   That nasty
    Fever's fault, that quite amazingly   3360
    Affects the nerves. Eh, Princess?
QUEEN: I did want
    So much to visit you, my Love—But that
    Is not allowed.
OLIVAREZ: The Princess Eboli
    Did not at least lack for companionship—
QUEEN: I can imagine. But what is the matter?
    You're trembling.
EBOLI: Nothing—nothing in the least,
    My Queen. I beg permission to retire.
QUEEN: You are concealing something from us, are
    More ill indeed than you would have us think.

128

And you find standing difficult. Come, help   3370
Her, Countess, to sit down upon this stool.
EBOLI: In the fresh air I will feel better.
                        (*Exit.*)
QUEEN: Follow
Her, Countess—What an odd attack!
            (*A page enters and speaks with the Duchess,
                who then turns to the Queen.*)
OLIVAREZ: Marquis
Of Posa waits, Your Majesty—He is
Sent by His Majesty the King.
QUEEN: I shall
Receive him here.
        (*The page goes out and opens the door
        for the Marquis. The Marquis falls on one
        knee before the Queen, who gives him a
        sign to rise.*)
                        What is my lord's command?
May it be publicly—
MARQUIS: My errand is
Directed to Your Royal Majesty alone.
                    (*The ladies withdraw at a sign from
                            the Queen.*)
QUEEN: (*full of astonishment*)
What's this? Can I believe my eyes, Marquis?
The King sends you to me on errands?
MARQUIS: Does   3380
Your Majesty find that so odd? To me
It does not seem so in the least.
QUEEN: The world
Is thrown out of its orbit. You and *he*—
I must confess—
MARQUIS: That it sounds curious?
That may well be—The present time is still
Prolific with its varied miracles.
QUEEN: None greater, scarcely.

MARQUIS: Well, suppose that I
  Had let myself be finally converted—
  Were tired of playing odd man at the court
  Of Philip? Odd man! What is that? Whoever   3390
  Would be of use to human beings must
   Try first to make himself the equal of them.
  What good is ostentatious dress of sects?
  Suppose—Who is so free from vanity
  As not to proselytize for his beliefs?—
  Suppose I entertained the notion of
  Transposing mine upon a throne?
QUEEN: No!—No,
  Marquis. I should not even as a jest
  Like to accuse you of that immature
  Fancy. You are not the dreamer to   3400
  Begin what cannot be concluded.
MARQUIS: That,
  I think, is just the question now.
QUEEN: The most
  I might accuse you of, Marquis,—what might
  Almost surprise me in you, would be—would be—
MARQUIS: Equivocation. May be.
QUEEN: Least of all
  Insincerity. The King did not
  Apparently wish you to tell me what
  You are about to tell me.
MARQUIS: No.
QUEEN: And can
  The good cause dignify the evil means?
  Your noble pride—forgive me for this doubt—   3410
  Can it be lent thus to this office? I
  Should hardly think so—
MARQUIS: Nor should *I*, if here
  The object were but to deceive the King.
  Such is not my intention, though. This time
  I mean to serve him more sincerely than

He has enjoined me.

QUEEN: There I recognize you,
And now that is enough! What is he doing?

MARQUIS: The King?—As things look now, I shall quite soon
Have my revenge upon my austere judge.
The news I am in no great hurry to   3420
Relate, Your Majesty, it seems to me,
Is in still less, yes, far less of a hurry
To hear—And yet it must be heard! The Monarch
Bids me entreat Your Majesty to grant
No audience to the Ambassador
Of France today. That was my errand. It
Is finished now.

QUEEN: And that is all, Marquis,
That you have to announce to me from him?

MARQUIS: That is approximately everything
That justifies my being here.

QUEEN: I shall   3430
Content myself, Marquis, with ignorance of
What must perhaps remain a mystery
To me—

MARQUIS: Yes, that it *must,* my Queen.—Were you
Not *you,* however, I should hasten to
Give you instruction in some matters, warn
You on the score of certain persons,—but
With you that is not necessary. Danger
May appear and disappear around you,
And you not be aware of it. All this
Is hardly worth dislodgment, after all,   3440
Of golden slumber from an angel's brow.
And this was not the thing that brought me here.
Prince Carlos—

QUEEN: O, how did you leave him?

MARQUIS: As
The only wise man of his time for whom
It is a crime to worship truth—and just

As doughtily prepared to die for *his*
Love as the other is to die for his.
I bring you but few words from him—but here
He is himself.

>   (*He gives the Queen a letter.*)

QUEEN: (*after reading it*)

>   He says he must see me.

MARQUIS: So I say also.

QUEEN: Will it make him happy   3450
If he sees with his own eyes that I am
Not happy either?

MARQUIS: No—but it will make him
More energetic and decisive.

QUEEN: How?

MARQUIS: The Duke of Alba has been named for Flanders.

QUEEN: Named—so I hear.

MARQUIS: Revoke that nomination
The King can never do. We know the King.
But it is also true: the Prince must not
Stay here—not here, especially now—and Flanders
Must not be sacrificed.

QUEEN: You know how to
Prevent that?

MARQUIS: Yes—perhaps. The remedy   3460
Is almost as bad as the peril. It
Is rash to desperation.—All the same,
I know no other way.

QUEEN: Name it.

MARQUIS: To you,
To you alone, my Queen, I am so bold
As to discover it. From you alone
Can Carlos hear it, hear it without horror.
The name which it will bear, to be quite frank,
Sounds somewhat harsh—

QUEEN: Rebellion—

MARQUIS: He is to

Be disobedient to the King, is to
Make his way secretly to Brussels, where   3470
With open arms the Flemish people will
Be waiting for him. All the Netherlands
Will rise up at his watchword. The good cause
Takes strength from a king's son. There let him set
The Spanish throne a-tremble by his arms.
What formerly the father in Madrid
Refused him, he will grant in Brussels.
QUEEN: You have spoken
With him today, and make this claim?
MARQUIS: Because
I spoke with him today.
QUEEN: *(after a pause)*   The plan you show
Me frightens and—delights me too. I think   3480
You are not wrong—The notion is a bold
One, and that is just why, I think,
It pleases me. I shall let it mature.
But does the Prince know of it?
MARQUIS: My plan was
That he should first hear of it from your lips.
QUEEN: Without a doubt! The plan is excellent—
Unless the Prince's youth—
MARQUIS: Will do no harm.
He will find there an Egmont and an Orange,
The gallant warriors of Emperor Charles,
As shrewd in council as redoubted in   3490
The field.
QUEEN: *(with vivacity)*
          No! The idea is both lofty
And fine—The Prince must act. I feel that keenly.
Here in Madrid the role he is seen acting
Is crushing me down to the ground for his
Sake—France I promise him; Savoy as well.
I quite agree with you, Marquis, he must
Act.—But this venture calls for money.

MARQUIS: That is also
    Laid by.
QUEEN: And I know ways besides.
MARQUIS: Then I
    May give him hope for the encounter?
QUEEN: I
    Shall think it over.
MARQUIS: Carlos urges for   3500
    An answer now, Your Majesty—and I
    Have promised not to come back emptyhanded.
            (*handing his writing tablets to the Queen*)
    Two lines will be enough for now—
QUEEN: (*after writing*)   Shall I
    See you again?
MARQUIS: Whenever you command.
QUEEN: Whenever I—whenever I command?
    Marquis! How am I to construe this freedom?
MARQUIS: As guilelessly as *you* are able to.
    We do enjoy it, that suffices—that
    Suffices for my Queen.
QUEEN: (*breaking the thought*) How happy I
    Would be, Marquis, if only Freedom might   3510
    Be spared that place of refuge yet in Europe!
    And if it should be spared because of *him!*—
    Count on my silent sympathy—
MARQUIS: (*with ardor*)   O, I
    Was sure I would find understanding here—
            (*The Duchess Olivarez appears at the door.*)
QUEEN: (*distantly to the Marquis*)
    What has come from my lord the King I shall
    Revere as though it were a law. Go and
    Give him assurance of my acquiescence.
                    (*She gives him a sign.
                    The Marquis leaves.*)

SCENE 2

A gallery.
Don Carlos and Count Lerma.

CARLOS: Here we shall be quite undisturbed. What have
You to reveal to me?

LERMA: Your Highness used
To have a friend here in this court.

LERMA: (*startled*)   Not that   3520
I knew of!—What? What are you driving at?

LERMA: Then I must beg you to forgive me for
Discovering more than I was supposed to.
However, for Your Highness' peace of mind,
I have it from a loyal hand at least;
In short, I have it from myself.

CARLOS: About
Whom are you speaking?

LERMA: Marquis Posa—

CARLOS: Well?

LERMA: If there should be a little something more
Known of Your Highness than a person should
Know, as I am inclined to fear—

CARLOS: As you   3530
Fear?

LERMA: —He was with the King.

CARLOS: So?

LERMA: Two whole hours,
In very secret conversation.

CARLOS: Really?

LERMA: It was not talk of trivialities.

CARLOS: That I can well believe.

LERMA: I heard your name,
Prince, mentioned rather frequently.

CARLOS: That is,
I hope, not a bad sign.

LERMA: Again this morning
In the bed chamber of His Majesty
The Queen was mentioned most mysteriously.
CARLOS: *(stepping back in dismay)*
Count Lerma?
LERMA: And when the Marquis had left,   3540
I received the order to admit
Him henceforth unannounced.
CARLOS: That is indeed
A great deal.
LERMA: Quite unprecedented, Prince,
So far as I recall, since I have served
The King.
CARLOS: A great deal!—And, how did you say,
How was there mention of the Queen?
LERMA: *(falling back)*   No, Prince,
No! That is counter to my loyalty.
CARLOS: How odd! You tell me one thing and conceal
The other from me.
LERMA: One I owed to you,
The other I owe to the Monarch.
CARLOS: —You
Are right.
LERMA: I have consistently, of course,   3550
Known the Marquis to be a man of honor.
CARLOS: Then you have known him very well.
LERMA: All virtue
Is stainless—till the moment of the test.
CARLOS: That is true here and still quite true hereafter.
LERMA: The favor of a great King is, I think,
Open to question. On that golden hook
Has many a stout virtue bled to death.
CARLOS: O yes.
LERMA: And often it is even prudent to
Reveal what can no longer be kept secret.
CARLOS: Yes! Prudent! But, as you say, have you known   3560

The Marquis solely as a man of honor?

LERMA: If he *still* is, my doubt will render him
No worse, and you, my Prince, win double.

(*He starts to go.*)

CARLOS: (*follows him, touched, and presses his hand.*)

I

Win triple, noble, worthy man—I see
Myself one friend the richer, and it does
Not cost me the one that I had.

(*Exit Lerma.*)

(*The Marquis Posa comes through
the gallery.*)

MARQUIS: Charles! Charles!

CARLOS: Who calls? Oh! It is you! Quite right. I'll hurry
On to the monastery. Follow soon.

(*He starts to leave.*)

MARQUIS: Two minutes only—wait.

CARLOS: But what if someone
Should find us—

MARQUIS: They won't. It is quickly done.   3570
The Queen—

CARLOS: You have been with my father?

MARQUIS: Yes,
He had me summoned.

CARLOS: (*full of expectation*)   Well?

MARQUIS: It is all right.
You will see her.

CARLOS: And what about the King?
What did the King want?

MARQUIS: He? Not much—He was
Just curious to find out who I was—
Good friends unasked had been officious. How
Do I know? He proposed that I should enter
His service.

CARLOS: You declined?

MARQUIS: Of course.

CARLOS: On what
Terms did you separate?
MARQUIS: Quite good.
CARLOS: There was
Not any mention, I suppose, of me? 3580
MARQUIS: Of you? Why, yes. In general.
              (*He takes out his letter case
              and gives it to the Prince.*)
              Here for now
Are two words from the Queen. Tomorrow I
Shall find out where and how—
CARLOS: (*reads very absentmindedly, puts the paper in
    his pocket, and starts to go.*)
              So you will meet
Me at the Prior's.
MARQUIS: Wait. Why are you in
Such haste? No one is coming.
CARLOS: (*with feigned smile*) Have we really
Exchanged our roles? You are astonishingly
Sure of yourself today.
MARQUIS: Today? But why
Today?
CARLOS: And what does the Queen write to me?
MARQUIS: Did you not read it just this minute?
CARLOS: I?
Oh, yes.
MARQUIS: What is the matter? What is wrong? 3590
CARLOS: (*reads the letter again. Enraptured and ardent*)
Angel of Heaven! Yes! I will—I will—
I will be worthy of you—Love makes great
Souls greater. Let it be what it may be.
If *you* require it of me, I obey.—
She writes that I am to prepare myself
To make some great decision. What can she
Have meant by that? Do you know?
MARQUIS: Even if

I knew, Charles,—are you in the frame of mind
To hear it now?
CARLOS: Have I offended you?
I was distraught. Forgive me, Roderick.   3600
MARQUIS: Distraught? By what?
CARLOS: By—I don't know myself.
This letter case is mine then?
MARQUIS: Not entirely.
Or rather, I had come, in fact, to ask
For yours.
CARLOS: For mine! What for?
MARQUIS: And for whatever
You might have in the way of trifles which
Should not fall in the hands of a third party,
Or in the way of letters or rough drafts
You might be carrying—in short, for your
Whole letter case.
CARLOS: But why?
MARQUIS: Just for emergencies.
Who can give guarantee against surprise?   3610
No one will look for them wtih me. Give them
To me.
CARLOS: (*very uneasy*)
          But this is odd! Why suddenly
This—
MARQUIS: Have no fear. I did not mean to hint
At anything. Of course not. This is caution
Before the danger comes. I did not mean,
I truly did not mean you should be frightened.
CARLOS: (*gives him the letter case.*)
Guard it well.
MARQUIS: I will.
CARLOS: (*gives him a pointed look*) O Roderick!
It is a great deal that I give.
MARQUIS: Not nearly
So much as I already have from you—

The rest when we meet *there*. And now farewell—   3620
Farewell.
                    (*He starts to leave.*)
CARLOSS   (*struggles dubiously with himself. Finally he calls him
      back.*)
                    Give me the letters back again.
There is among them one from her, that she
Wrote to me in Alcala at the time
When I was lying ill and close to death,
And I have always worn it by my heart.
To part with it is hard for me. Leave me
That letter—just that one—take all the rest.
                    (*He removes it and hands back the
                              letter case.*)
MARQUIS: Charles, I am loath to do it. That is just
The one I want.
CARLOS: Farewell!
      (*He walks away slowly and silently. At the door he stops for
      a moment, turns, and brings the letter to him.*)
                              There, now you have it.
      (*His hand trembles, tears well in his eyes, he falls upon the
      Marquis' neck and presses his face against his bosom.*)
This cannot be my father's doing? Can it,   3630
My Roderick? He can't be doing *this*?
                    (*He walks rapidly away.*)
MARQUIS: (*looking after him in astonishment*)
Could it be possible? Could it? Could I
Have failed to know him? Wholly know him? Could
That fold have really been there in his heart
Toward me? Does he mistrust his friend?
No! It is blasphemy!—What has he done
That I accuse him of the weakest weakness?
What I accuse him of, I am myself—
Surprise him—that it may, I can imagine.
When had he looked for this odd reticence   3640
On the part of his friend?—And hurt him too!

But that I cannot spare you, Charles, and I
Must longer still keep your good heart in torment.
The King put his faith in the vessel to
Which he entrusted his most sacred secret;
Faith calls for gratitude. What good would come
Of idle chatter if my silence will
Do you no harm? Saves you, perhaps, from harm?
Why show a sleeping man the thunder cloud
That hangs above his head?—It will suffice   3650
For me to guide it quietly on past you,
And when you wake, there the bright sky will be.

(Exit.)

SCENE 3

The King's study.
The King in an armchair; beside him the Infanta Clara
Eugenia.

KING: (*after a profound silence*)
No! she is after all my daughter—How
Can Nature lie with such veracity?
Why, these blue eyes are surely mine! Do I
Not see myself again in every feature?
Child of my love, you are, you are—I clasp
You to my heart—you are my flesh and blood.
                    (*He stops short and is silent.*)
My flesh and blood! What worse thing can I fear?
My features, are they not *his* features too?   3660
    (*He has picked up the medallion and keeps looking alter-*
    nately at the picture and at a mirror which stands op-
    posite. Finally he throws it on the floor, gets up quickly,
    and thrusts the Infanta away.)
Away! Away! In this abyss I perish.

(Enter Count Lerma.)

LERMA: Her Majesty the Queen has just appeared
Out in the antechamber.

KING: Now?

LERMA: And asks
Most graciously for audience.

KING: Right now?
Now? At this unaccustomed hour?—No!
I cannot see her now—not now—

LERMA: Here is
Her Majesty herself—

(Exit.)

*(Enter the Queen. The Infanta flies to meet her and nestles
    at her side. The Queen falls on her knees before the
    King, who stands silent and confused.)*

QUEEN: My lord and husband—
I must—I am compelled to come before
Your throne in order to implore for justice.

KING: For justice—

QUEEN: I discover I have met   3670
Unworthy treatment at this court.
My jewel casket has been rifled—

KING: What?

QUEEN: Things of great worth to me are missing from it—

KING: Things of great worth to you—

QUEEN: With allegation
That some unwitting fellow's impudence
Was able—

KING: Allegation—impudence—
But—Stand up.

QUEEN: No, my husband, not until
You have bound yourself with a promise, by
Force of your royal arm, to place the miscreant
Before me for my satisfaction, or,   3680
If not, then to remove me from a court

That keeps my thief concealed—
KING: But do stand up—
   In this position—Stand up—
QUEEN: (rising)   That he must
   Be of some rank, I know—for in the casket
   Were pearls and diamonds of much beyond
   The value of a million, whereas he
   Was satisfied with letters—
KING: Which I must—
QUEEN: Most willingly, my husband. There were letters
   And a medallion with the Prince's picture.
KING: With—
QUEEN: The Infante, with your son.
KING: To you?   3690
QUEEN: To me.
KING: With the Infante! You say that
   To *me*?
QUEEN: Why not say that to you, my husband?
KING: With that look on your face?
QUEEN: What startles you?
   I think you will recall the letters which
   Don Carlos wrote to me at Saint Germain
   With the approval of both crowns. Though whether
   The picture that he sent along with them
   Was meant to be included in that freedom,
   Or whether his rash hopes permitted him
   That bold step independently,—these things   3700
   I shall not undertake to judge. If it
   Was over-haste, it was most pardonable—
   On that point I shall be his guarantee!
   For it had not occurred to him at that time
   It would be for his mother—
             (*She notices a movement of the King's.*)
                        What is this?
What is the matter?

THE INFANTA: (*who meanwhile has found the medallion on the floor and has been playing with it, brings it to the Queen.*)

                  Look what I have, mother!
The pretty picture—

QUEEN: What, my—
   (*She recognizes the medallion and stops in speechless rigidity. Both look at each other with unaverted gaze. After a long silence*)

                    Really, Sire!
I find *this* means of testing one's wife's heart
A very royal, noble one—But I
Should like to be allowed one further question.   3710

KING: It is for me to question.

QUEEN: Innocence
Must not be made to suffer on account
Of my suspicion. If this theft was done
At your command—

KING: It was.

QUEEN: Then I have no one to
Accuse and no one else to pity—no one
But *you,* whose lot was not to have a wife
With whom such tactics would be worth your while.

KING: This kind of talk I know—But, Madam,
Not for a second time shall it deceive me
As it deceived me in Aranjuez.   3720
That Queen of angel purity who then
Made her defense with so much dignity—
I know her better now.

QUEEN: What's this?

KING: In brief
And barring reservations, Madam!—Is
It true, still true, you spoke with no one there?
With no one? Is that really true?

QUEEN: I did speak there
With the Infante. Yes.

KING: Yes?—Now it all
  Comes out. It is quite clear. So insolent!
  So little care about my honor!
QUEEN: Honor, Sire?
  If any honor was to be offended,   3730
  I fear a greater one was risked than what
  Castile had fetched me as a wedding gift.
KING: Why did you disavow it to me?
QUEEN: For
  The reason, Sire, that I am not accustomed
  To be interrogated in the presence
  Of courtiers as a malefactor. Truth
  I never shall deny when it is asked for
  With deference and gentleness—And was
  That how Your Majesty addressed me in
  Aranjuez? Is an assemblage of   3740
  The whole nobility the seat of judgment
  Before which queens shall be haled up to render
  An accounting for their private actions?
  I had on that occasion granted to
  The Prince an audience which he had requested
  Most urgently. I had so done, my husband,
  Because I so desired—because I do
  Not wish to set up usage as the judge
  Of things that I consider innocent—
  And I concealed it from you for the reason   3750
  That I had no desire to argue with
  Your Majesty before my court about
  That freedom.
KING: You speak very boldly, Madam—
QUEEN: And I shall add, because the Prince has scarcely
  The pleasure of that sanction in his father's
  Heart which he deserves—
KING: Which he deserves?
QUEEN: Why should I make a secret of it, Sire?
  I cherish him extremely and I love

Him as my dearest relative, who once
Had been deemed worthy to assume a name 3760
That touched me closer—I have not yet learned
To comprehend that he should be more alien
To me than any other just because
He formerly had been more dear to me
Than any other. If your policies
Of state establish ties as they see fit,
Then it shall be somewhat more difficult
For them to disestablish them again.
I will not hate just whom I am supposed to—
And, since I have been forced to speak at last— 3770
I will not have it any longer—will
Not have my free choice bound—

KING: Elizabeth!
You have beheld me in my hours of weakness.
That memory makes you thus bold. You trust
In an omnipotence that you have often
Enough put to the test against my firmness—
But fear the more. The thing that has brought me
To weakness, can lead me to frenzy also.

QUEEN: What crime have I committed?

KING: (*taking her hand*)   If it is,
Is *after all*—and is it not already?— 3780
If the complete and heaped up measure of
Your guilt is added to by one breath's weight—
If I have been betrayed—

                    (*He releases her hand.*)
                              I can prevail
In triumph over this last weakness also.
I can and will—but woe to me and you,
Elizabeth!

QUEEN: What crime have I committed?

KING: For my part then let blood be shed—

QUEEN: Have things

Gone that far?

KING: I no longer know
Myself—I do not honor any custom
Or any voice of Nature any more,   3790
Or any pact of nations—

QUEEN: How I pity
Your Majesty—

KING: (*losing his self-control*)
                    You pity me! The pity
Of an adulteress—

THE INFANTA: (*clings to her mother in terror.*)
                    The King is angry, and
My lovely mother weeps.
                    (*The King thrusts the child roughly
                    away from the Queen.*)

QUEEN: (*with gentleness and dignity but with trembling voice*)
                    I must remove
This child to safety from mistreatment. Come
With me, my daughter.
                    (*She takes her into her arms.*)
                    If the King refuses
To know you any longer I must send
Beyond the Pyrenees and have defenders
Come to take up our cause.
                    (*She starts to leave.*)

KING: (*startled*)   Queen?!

QUEEN: I can stand
No more of this—this is too much—   3800
                    (*She is about to reach the door and
                    collapses upon the threshold.*)

KING: (*rushing up full of dismay*)
My God! My God! What is this?—

THE INFANTA: (*crying in terror*)   Oh, my mother
Is bleeding!
                    (*She rushes out.*)

KING: *(anxiously occupied with her)*
> What a frightful mischance! Blood!
Do I deserve so harsh a punishment
From you? Get up. Come to your senses. Stand
Up! There are people coming! They will see us—
Stand up—Is my whole court to feast its eyes
Upon this spectacle? Must I implore
You to get up?
> *(She rises, supported by the King.)*
> *(Enter Alba and Domingo, frightened.*
>   *Ladies follow.)*
>   Have the Queen taken home.
She is not well.
> *(Exit the Queen, accompanied by the*
> *ladies. Alba and Domingo come closer.)*

ALBA: The Queen in tears, and blood
Upon her face—

KING: Does that amaze the devils   3810
Who have misled me?

ALBA AND DOMINGO: We?

KING: Who said enough
To bring me to the point of madness; but
As for convincing me, said nothing.

ALBA: We
Gave what we had—

KING: May Hell reward you. I
Have done a thing that I regret. Was that
The language of a guilty conscience?

MARQUIS OF POSA: *(still offstage)*   Is
The Monarch to be seen?

KING: *(starting up with animation at the sound of the voice)*
> Ah! There he is!
> *(advancing several steps to meet*
>   *the Marquis)*
Ah, you are welcome here, Marquis—Duke, I

Now have no further need of you. Leave us.
                    (*Alba and Domingo look at each*
                     other in mute amazement and go.)
MARQUIS: Sire, it is hard for that old man, who marched   3820
Toward death in twenty battles for your sake,
To see himself dismissed that way.
KING: It well
Befits that you think *so,* and I act *so.*
What you have been to me for these few hours
He never has been in a lifetime. I
Have no wish to be secretive about my favor;
The token of my royal preference
Shall shine out clear and far upon your brow.
I want the man whom I have chosen as
My friend to be well envied.
MARQUIS: Even if   3830
The cloak of darkness only made him able
To merit such a name?
KING: What do
You bring me?
MARQUIS: Passing through the antechamber
Just now I heard a frightful rumor which
Seemed unbelievable—A violent
Exchange of words—and blood—the Queen—
KING: You come from *there?*
MARQUIS: I would be horrified
If the report were not untrue, if on
Your Majesty's part something meanwhile should
Perhaps have happened—I have made important   3840
Discoveries that change the state of matters
Entirely.
KING: Well?
MARQUIS: I found occasion to
Remove the Prince's letter case together
With certain papers which, it is my hope,

Will shed some light—
                    (*He gives the King Carlos's letter case.*)
KING: (*going through it eagerly*)
                              A letter from the Emperor,
My father—How is this? about which I
Do not remember ever having heard?
                    (*He reads it through, lays it aside,
                    and hurries on to other papers.*)
The project of a fortress—Excerpts of
Ideas out of Tacitus—And what
Would this be?—I should know this hand!   3850
A lady sent it, certainly. "This key——"
                    (*He reads attentively, now aloud,
                              now inaudibly.*)
"The farther chambers of the Queen's pavilion"—
What's this?—"Here love may make confession free—
Requitement—for the modest sufferer, reward"—
Satanic treachery! I recognize
It now. She is the one. It is her hand!
MARQUIS: The Queen's? That is impossible—
KING: The Princess
Of Eboli's—
MARQUIS: So then it would be true
What Henarez the page confessed to me
Not long ago, who brought the key and letter.   3860
KING: (*taking the Marquis' hand, in vehement emotion*)
Marquis, I see myself in dreadful hands!
This woman—I acknowledge it—Marquis,
This woman forced the jewel casket of
The Queen, and the first warning came from her—
Who knows how much the monk may know about it—
I have been taken in by a vile trick.
MARQUIS: Then it is lucky that—
KING: Marquis! Marquis!
I now begin to fear that I have done

My wife excessive wrong—
MARQUIS: If there has ever
  Been any kind of secret understandings   3870
  Between the Prince and Queen, they certainly
  Have had a purport far—far different
  From what they have accused her of. I have
  Reliable reports the Prince's wish
  To leave for Flanders had its origin
  In the Queen's mind.
KING: I always thought it did.
MARQUIS: The Queen has her ambition—May I go
  On to say more?—With sensitivity
  She sees herself deceived in her proud hopes,
  Excluded from participation in   3880
  The throne. The Prince's fiery youth presented
  Itself to her far-seeing plans—her heart—
  I doubt if she can love.
KING: Her tricks of statecraft
  Have nothing that could make me tremble.
MARQUIS: And as to whether she is loved—or whether
  Worse is not to be feared from the Infante:
  This question would seem worth investigating.
  Here stricter vigilance, I think, is needed—
KING: You shall be warrant for him—
MARQUIS: (after some deliberation)   If Your Majesty
  Believes me capable of carrying out   3890
  This office, I must beg that you transmit
  It wholly to my hands without conditions.
KING: That shall be done.
MARQUIS: At least without disturbance
  From any helper, by whatever name
  He may be called, in undertakings which
  I might perhaps find necessary to—
KING: From none. I promise you. You have been my
  Good angel. How much gratitude I owe

You for this hint!
          (*to Lerma who comes in at these last words*)
                    How did you leave the Queen?
LERMA: Still very much exhausted from her fainting spell.   3900
    (*He looks at the Marquis with ambiguous*
                    glances and leaves.)
MARQUIS: (*after a pause, to the King*)
    One more precaution seems required.
    The Prince, I fear, may possibly get warnings.
    He has good friends a-plenty—and perhaps
    Connections with the rebels up in Ghent.
    Fear might lead him to desperate decisions—
    Therefore I would advise the taking of
    Immediate preventive measures to
    Offset that chance by rapid means.
KING: You are
    Quite right. But how—
MARQUIS: A secret order for
    Detention, which Your Majesty might place   3910
    In my hands, to be used immediately
    The very instant danger seems to threaten—
                    (*as the King seems to be dubious*)
    And—first of all, it would remain a secret
    Of state until—
KING: (*going to the writing desk and writing out the order for*
    detention)
                    The Empire is at stake—
    Extraordinary means are sanctioned by the urgent
    Danger—Here, Marquis—I do not need
    To recommend that you show no indulgence—
MARQUIS: (*takes the order for detention.*)
    It will be for a last resort, my King.
KING: (*lays his hand on his shoulder.*)
    Go, go, my dear Marquis—and bring me back
    Sleep to my nights and quiet to my heart.   3920
        (*Exeunt both in opposite directions.*)

SCENE 4

A gallery.
Enter Carlos in extreme anxiety, and Count Lerma to meet him.

CARLOS: I was just looking for you.
LERMA: And I you.
CARLOS: Can it be true? For God's sake, is it true?
LERMA: What?
CARLOS: That he drew a dagger on her? that
   She was removed all bloody from his room?
   By all the saints! Give me an answer. What
   Should I believe? What is the truth?
LERMA: She fell
   Into a faint and scratched herself in falling.
   No more than that.
CARLOS: There is no other danger?
   No other? On your honor, Count?
LERMA: Not for
   The Queen—for you, however, all the more.   3930
CARLOS: None for my mother! Well, thank God for that!
   A ghastly rumor reached my ears that claimed
   The King was raging at both child and mother,
   And that a secret was discovered.
LERMA: It
   May be that last is true—
CARLOS: True? How?
LERMA: I have already given you *one* warning
   Today, Prince, which you scorned. Make better use
   Of this one now.
CARLOS: What?
LERMA: If I am not much
   Mistaken, Prince, I saw in your hands just

The other day a letter case made of 3940
A sky-blue velvet worked with gold—

CARLOS: *(rather startled)* I do
Own one like that. Yes—Well?—

LERMA: A silhouette,
I think, was on the cover, set in pearls—

CARLOS: Quite right.

LERMA: When I stepped into the King's study
Quite unexpectedly just now, I thought
I saw that very one in his hand, and
There with him Marquis Posa stood—

CARLOS: *(after a short numbed silence, vehemently)*
That is
Not true.

LERMA: *(touchily)* Then I am frankly a deceiver.

CARLOS: *(looks at him for a long time.)*
Yes. That you are.

LERMA: O, I forgive you that!

CARLOS: *(walks up and down in fearful agitation and finally
stops facing him.)*
What has he done to harm you? Or what have 3950
Our guiltless ties of friendship done to harm you,
That you should strive with hellish eagerness
To rend them thus asunder?

LERMA: Prince, I honor
The sorrow which makes you unfair.

CARLOS: O God!—
God!—God!—Preserve me from suspicion!

LERMA: Also
I well recall just what the King's words were.
As I stepped in he was just saying: "How
Much gratitude I owe you for this hint!"

CARLOS: Be still! Be still!

LERMA: They say the Duke of Alba
Has fallen—and that from Prince Ruy Gomez 3960

The Great Seal has been taken and awarded
To the Marquis—
CARLOS: (*lost in profound brooding*)
                    And this he did not mention to me!
Why did he not do so?
LERMA: The whole court marvels
At him already as a minister
All-powerful and as a favorite
Unlimited—
CARLOS: He once was fond of me.
I was as dear to him as his own soul.
O, that I know—A thousand proofs have proved it.
But shall not millions, shall the fatherland
Not be more dear to him than one alone?   3970
His heart was too great for a single friend,
And Carlos' fortune too small for his love.
He sacrificed me to his virtue. Can
I blame him for it?—Oh yes, it is certain!
Now it is certain. I have lost him now.
            (*He turns aside and covers his face.*)
LERMA: (*after a silence*)
What can I do for you, my best of Princes?
CARLOS: (*without looking at him*)
You can go to the King and sell me to him.
I have no gifts to give you.
LERMA: Do you want
To wait and see what may ensue?
CARLOS: (*braces himself against the balustrade and stares fixedly
    ahead.*)
                              I have
Lost him. Now I am utterly alone!   3980
LERMA: (*approaches him with sympathetic emotion.*)
You do not want to think about your safety?
CARLOS: About my safety?—Good, kind man!
LERMA: And have

You no one else for whom to tremble? No one?

CARLOS: (*starting up*)

My God! What you remind me of!—My mother!
The letter I gave back to him! first would
Not let him have, then gave him after all!

> (*He paces up and down, wringing his hands
> in vehement emotion.*)

How could *she* have deserved it of him? He
Ought to have spared *her*. Lerma, shouldn't he?

> (*impetuously, with decision*)

O I must go to her—must warn her, must
Prepare her for this—Lerma, my dear Lerma—   3990
Whom shall I send? Do I have no one left?
Praise God! There is *one* friend yet—Things there can
Be made no worse.

> (*Exit rapidly.*)

LERMA: (*follows him and calls after him.*)

> Where are you going, Prince?

> (*Exit.*)

SCENE 5

A room in the Queen's apartments.
The Queen, Alba, Domingo.

ALBA: If we may have the privilege, great Queen—

QUEEN: What can I do for you?

DOMINGO: Sincere concern about
Your Royal Majesty's exalted person
Will not allow us to be idly silent
Concerning an occurrence which bears threat

Against your safety.

ALBA: We are hurrying
To bring our timely warning and disarm   4000
A plot which is now being played against you—
DOMINGO: And to lay down our zeal—our services
As well—at the feet of Your Majesty.
QUEEN: *(looks at them in astonishment.)*
Most reverend Sir, and you, my noble Duke,
You take me by surprise indeed. Of such
Devotion to me from Domingo and
Duke Alba I had really no idea.
I realize how much it must be prized—
You tell me of a plot that threatens me.
May I be told who—
ALBA: We would urge you to   4010
Be on your guard against a Marquis Posa,
Who is engaged in secret errands for
His Majesty the King.
QUEEN: I learn with pleasure
How good a choice the King has made. I long
Have heard the Marquis praised as a great man
And as a noble human being. Never
Was that supreme award bestowed more justly—
DOMINGO: Bestowed more justly? We know better.
ALBA: It
Has long since ceased to be a secret, what
This man has let himself be used for.
QUEEN: What?   4020
What could that be? You have my expectations
Stretched taut.
DOMINGO: Is it a long time since
Your Majesty last had occasion to look into
Your jewel-casket?
QUEEN: What?
DOMINGO: And found that nothing

Was missing there among the precious things?
QUEEN: How so? What I have missed, the whole court knows.—
  But Marquis Posa? What connection does
  The Marquis Posa have with all of this?
ALBA: Quite close, Your Majesty—for missing also
  Are some important papers of the Prince's,   4030
  Which have been seen this very morning in
  The King's hands—when the cavalier had had
  A private audience.
QUEEN: *(after some reflection)* Most odd, by Heaven!
  Extremely odd!—I find an enemy
  Confronting me whom I had never dreamed of,
  And on the other hand two friends whom I cannot
  Remember ever having had.—For really,
           (as she directs a penetrating glance
               at both of them)
  I must confess that, as for that disservice
  Which had been done me with my lord, I was
  Inclined to lay it to your charge.
ALBA: Our charge?   4040
QUEEN: To both of you.
DOMINGO: Duke Alba! Us!
QUEEN: *(her eyes still fixed on them)* How glad
  I am to be aware so soon of my
  Excessive haste—In any case, I had
  Decided to request His Majesty
  This very day to summon my accuser
  Before me. All the better now. I can
  Invoke the Duke of Alba's testimony.
ALBA: Mine? Would you do that seriously?
QUEEN: Why not?
DOMINGO: Invalidating all the service we
  Have done you secretly—
QUEEN: Done secretly?   4050
         (with pride and earnestness)

Duke Alba, I should really like to know
What things your King's wife would have to arrange
With you, or to arrange with you, Priest, which
Her husband might not know about—Am I
Then innocent or guilty?
DOMINGO: What a question!
ALBA: What if the King were not so just, however?
Or were not so at least just now?
QUEEN: Then I
Shall have to wait until he is—And when
He is, the winner will be fortunate!

> (*She makes them a bow and goes out. They*
> *withdraw in a different direction.*)

SCENE 6

The Princess of Eboli's apartments.
The Princess of Eboli is alone when suddenly Carlos appears.

EBOLI: It's true, then, this extraordinary piece of news   4060
Which has already filled the court?

> (*Enter Carlos.*)

CARLOS: Do not be frightened,
Princess! I shall be as gentle as
A child.
EBOLI: Prince—this surprise.
CARLOS: Then you are still
Offended? Still?
EBOLI: Prince!
CARLOS: (*more urgently*)   Are you still offended?
I beg you, tell me if you are.
EBOLI: What is this?

You seem to have forgotten, Prince—What have
You come for?
CARLOS: *(seizing her hand with vehemence)*
                    Can you hate forever, girl?
Will hurt love never pardon?
EBOLI: *(tries to wrench herself free.)*   What would you
Remind me of, Prince?
CARLOS: Of your kindness and
Of my ingratitude—O, I well know,   4070
Girl, that I hurt you deeply, lacerated
Your tender heart, and wrung tears out of those
Angelic eyes,—alas! and I am not
Here even now to tell you I repent it.
EBOLI: Prince, let me go—I—
CARLOS: I have come because
You are a gentle girl, because I count
Upon your beautiful and kindly soul.
You see, girl, I have no friends left in this
World any more but you alone. You once
Were fond of me—You will not always hate   4080
And be irreconcilable.
EBOLI: *(averting her face)*   Be still!
No more, in God's name, Prince—
CARLOS: Allow me to
Remind you of those golden times, allow
Me to remind you of your love, that love
Of yours against which I transgressed, girl, so
Unworthily. Allow me to make up
Now to you for what I have been to you
And for what your heart's dreams have given me—
Once more now—just once more set me before
Your heart as I then was, and to that image   4090
Make sacrifice of that which you can never
Sacrifice again in all of time.
EBOLI: O Charles, how cruelly you play with me!
CARLOS: Be greater than your sex. Forget offenses,

Do what no woman ever did before—
And what no woman after you will do.
I ask from you a thing unheard of—Let
Me—on my knees I beg you—let me speak
Just two words with my mother.
                    (*He throws himself at her feet.*)
                    (*The Marquis Posa rushes in with two
                    officers of the royal bodyguard behind him.*)
MARQUIS : (*out of breath, beside himself, stepping between them*)
                              What has he
Confessed? Do not believe him.
CARLOS :   (*still on his knees, his voice rising*)
                              By all you   4100
Hold sacred—
MARQUIS :   (*cutting him short, with vehemence*)
                    He is mad. Don't listen to
This raving man.
CARLOS :   (*louder, more urgently*)
                    It is a matter of
Life and death. O take me to her.
MARQUIS :   (*pulls the Princess away from him by force.*)
                              I
Will kill you if you listen to him.
                    (*to one of the officers*)
                              Count
Of Cordua. In the name of the Monarch.
          (*He shows him the order for detention.*)
The Prince is now your prisoner.
     (*Carlos stands rigid as though thunderstruck. The Princess
       emits a cry of fright and starts to flee. The officers are
       amazed. A long and profound pause. The Marquis is seen
       to be trembling violently and to be maintaining compo-
       sure with difficulty.*)
               (*to the Prince*) I must
Request your sword—You, Princess Eboli,
Will stay; and

(to one officer)
you will be my warrant that
His Highness speaks with no one—no one—not
With you yourself, on peril of your head.   4110
    (He speaks something further, softly, to
    the officer, then turns to the second one.)
I shall throw myself at the Monarch's feet
At once to justify this—
    (to Carlos) and to you—
You may expect me, Prince—within the hour.
    (Carlos allows himself to be led away without any sign of
    awareness. Only in passing does he cast a dull and dying
    look at the Marquis, who covers his face. The Princess
    attempts once more to flee; the Marquis seizes her by
    the arm and brings her back.)

EBOLI: In all the heavens' names, let me depart
From here—
MARQUIS: *(pulls her downstage, with fearful solemnity)*
    What did he tell you, wretched woman?
EBOLI: He told me nothing—Let me go—No, nothing—
MARQUIS: *(holding her back by force; more solemnly)*
How much did you find out? There is no more
Escape from here. In this world you will not
Repeat it to another soul.
EBOLI: *(looks into his face with terror.)*
    Great God!
What do you mean by that? You surely do   4120
Not mean to murder me?
MARQUIS: *(draws a dagger.)*   In fact, I am
Decidedly inclined to do so. Make
It short.
EBOLI: Me? Me? O Everlasting Mercy!
What crime have I committed?
MARQUIS: *(glancing toward heaven, the dagger poised*
    at her heart)
    There is still

Time left. The poison has not passed your lips
Yet. I shall smash the vessel, everything
Shall be just as it was—the fate of Spain,
A woman's life!—

> (*He stops, undecided, in this position.*)

EBOLI: (*has fallen to her knees beside him and is
looking steadfastly into his face.*)

> Well? Why do you still hesitate?

I do not ask for mercy—No! I have
Deserved to die, and wish to.

MARQUIS: (*lets his hand drop slowly. After brief
reflection*)

> That would be   4130

As cowardly as it is barbarous—
No! God be praised!—There is another way!

> (*He drops the dagger and hurries out. The Princess rushes
out through a different door.*)

SCENE 7

A room in the Queen's apartments.
The Queen is speaking to Countess Fuentes.

QUEEN: What is this uproar in the palace? Not
A noise today but terrifies me, Countess.
O do look into it and tell me what
It signifies.

> (*The Countess Fuentes goes out and
in rushes the Princess of Eboli.*)

EBOLI: (*breathless, pale, and distracted, sinking
down at the Queen's feet*)

> Help! Help! my Queen! He has

Been taken prisoner.

QUEEN: Who?

EBOLI: Marquis Posa
  Arrested him upon the King's command.

QUEEN: Arrested whom?

EBOLI: The Prince.

QUEEN: Are you insane?

EBOLI: They're taking him away right now.

QUEEN: And who   4140
  Arrested him?

EBOLI: The Marquis Posa.

QUEEN: Well!
  Praise be to God that it was the Marquis
  Who took him prisoner.

EBOLI: Can you say that
  So calmly, Queen? so coldly?—O my God!
  You have no notion—you don't know—

QUEEN: Why he
  Was taken prisoner?—Some misstep, I
  Imagine, which was quite in keeping with
  The youth's impulsive character.

EBOLI: Oh, no!
  No! I know better—No—O Queen! It was
  A villainous and devilish trick! There is   4150
  No rescue for him! He will die!

QUEEN: Will die!

EBOLI: And it was I who killed him!

QUEEN: He will die!
  Mad woman, have you lost your mind?

EBOLI: And why—
  Why will he die!—O if I could have known
  That it would come to this!

QUEEN: (takes her indulgently by the hand.)
                         O Princess, you
  Are still distraught. Collect your senses first,
  So that you can relate these things to me
  More calmly, not in ghastly images

That strike a horror to my inmost being.

What do you know? What is it that has happened?   4160

EBOLI: O not this condescension as from heaven,
  O not this kindness, Queen! Like flames of hell
  It strikes my conscience, searing as it strikes.
  I am not worthy to lift my unholy
  Gaze up to your glory. Trample down
  The wretched creature overwhelmed with shame,
  Remorse, and self-contempt who writhes here at
  Your feet.

QUEEN: Unhapy girl! What is it that
  You have to make confession of?

EBOLI: O angel
  Of light! O lofty saint! You neither know   4170
  Nor guess the devil on whom you have smiled
  So graciously—Be now apprised of him
  Today. I was the thief who robbed you.

QUEEN: You?

EBOLI: And it was I who took those letters to
  The King—

QUEEN: You?

EBOLI: Who had the audacity
  To make that accusation of you—

QUEEN: You—
  You could—

EBOLI: Revenge—and love—and frenzied madness—
  I was in love with the Infante and
  I hated you—

QUEEN: Because you were in love
  With him—?

EBOLI: Because I had confessed it to him   4180
  And found no love from him.

QUEEN: O everything
  Is now unriddled for me!—Rise. You loved him.
  I have forgiven you already. And already
  It is forgotten—Rise.

(She extends her arm to her.)

EBOLI: No! No! A frightful
  Confession still remains. No, not until,
  Great Queen—
QUEEN: *(attentively)* What more am I to hear? Go on—
EBOLI: The King—seduction—O avert your eyes—
  I read the condemnation in your face—
  The crime that I accused you of—I had
  Myself committed.
                    (She presses her burning face to the floor.)
                        (Exit the Queen.)
                        (A long pause.)
  *(After a few minutes the Duchess of Olivarez comes out of
    the chamber into which the Queen had gone and finds
    the Princess still lying in her former position. She ap-
    proaches her silently; at the sound, the latter rises and
    starts up like a mad woman when she perceives that the
    Queen is no longer there.)*
                    Heaven! She has left me.   4190
  Now all is over.
OLIVAREZ: *(comes closer to her.)* Princess Eboli—
EBOLI: I realize what you have come for, Duchess.
  The Queen has sent you in here to announce
  My sentence to me—Quickly, then!
OLIVAREZ: I have
  The order from Her Majesty to take
  Possession of your cross and of your keys—
EBOLI: *(as she takes a gold cross of an order from her
    bosom and places it in the hands of the
    Duchess)*
  But will it be vouchsafed to me to kiss
  Just *once* more the hand of the best of Queens?
OLIVAREZ: You will be told, once at the Mary Convent,
  What is determined in your case.
EBOLI: *(with tears welling)*   I shall   4200
  Not see the Queen again?

OLIVAREZ: (*embraces her with averted face.*)
                         Fare you with cheer.
(*She walks rapidly away. The Princess follows as far as the
door of the chamber, which is shut immediately after the
Duchess. For a few minutes she remains on her knees
before it, mute and motionless; then she rises suddenly
and rushes away with her face covered.*)
                (*Enter the Queen and the Marquis
                         of Posa.*)

QUEEN: At last, Marquis! How happy that you come!

MARQUIS: (*pale, his face distorted, his voice trembling,
    and throughout this scene in solemn and
    profound agitation*)
Your Majesty is quite alone? Can we
Be heard by anyone in these next rooms?

QUEEN: By no one—Why? What do you bring?
                (*as she looks at him more closely
                    and steps back, shocked*)
                                    And why
So wholly altered? What is this? You make
Me tremble, Marquis—all your features are
Disfigured like a dying man's—

MARQUIS: You know
Presumably—

QUEEN: That Charles has been arrested,
By you, in fact, they add—Then it is true?   4210
From any other person I would not
Believe it.

MARQUIS: It is true.

QUEEN: By you?

MARQUIS: By me.

QUEEN: (*looks at him dubiously for several minutes.*)
I do respect your actions even when
I do not comprehend them—This time though,
You must forgive the timid woman. I
Fear you are playing at a risky game.

MARQUIS: And I have lost it.

QUEEN: God in heaven!

MARQUIS: Be
    Quite calm, my Queen. For him provision has
    Been made. But I have lost it for *myself*.

QUEEN: What do I hear? My God!

MARQUIS: For who,   4220
    Who bade .ne hazard everything upon
    A doubtful throw? Yes, everything! or play
    So recklessly, in such self-confidence,
    With Heaven? Who is the man who thus presumes
    To steer the massive helm of Chance and yet
    Not be Omniscient God? O, it is proper!—
    But why precisely now of me? The moment
    Is precious as a human being's life!
    And who knows whether from the Judge's hand,
    That parsimonious hand, the final drops   4230
    Are not already falling for me?

QUEEN: From
    The Judge's hand?—But what a solemn tone!
    I do not understand what these words mean,
    But they fill me with terror—

MARQUIS: He is saved!
    It does not matter at what price! But for
    Today alone. He has few moments left.
    Let him be sparing of them. He must leave
    Madrid this very night.

QUEEN: This very night?

MARQUIS: Arrangements have been made. Within that same
    Carthusian monastery that has long   4240
    Since been the sanctuary of our friendship
    The post is waiting for him. Here in notes
    Is all that Luck has left me in this world.
    What is still lacking, *you* will add. I had,
    It's true, a great deal on my heart yet for
    My Charles, a great deal he should know; but I

May easily run short of leisure time
To settle everything with him in person—
You will see him this evening, so I turn
To you—

QUEEN: To give me peace of mind, Marquis,   4250
Explain yourself more clearly—do not talk
To me in such horrendous riddles—What
Has happened?

MARQUIS: I still have to make one more
Confession of importance; I depose
It in your hands. To me a happiness
Was granted such as only few have known:
I loved a ruler's son—My heart which had
Been dedicate to one alone, encompassed
The world entire!—Within my Carlos' soul
I shaped a paradise for millions. O,   4260
My dreams were beautiful—and yet it has
Pleased Providence to summon me before
My time away from my fair seeded fields.
Soon he will have his Roderick no more,
The friend yields place to the beloved. Here,
Here—here—upon this consecrated altar,
In the heart of his Queen I now depose
My final precious legacy; here let
Him find it when I am no more—
      (*He turns aside, tears choke his voice.*)

QUEEN: This is
The language of a dying man. I trust   4270
It is but agitation of your blood—
Or is there meaning in these words?

MARQUIS: (*has tried to get control of himself and continues
in a firmer tone.*)
                       Say to
The Prince that he is to recall the oath
Which in those days of high idealism
We swore together on the parted host.

Mine I have kept, and have been loyal to
It unto death—Now it is up to him
To keep his—
QUEEN: Unto death?
MARQUIS: Let him make real—
O tell him this—let him make real the dream.
That bold dream—vision of a newer state,   4280
The god-like offspring of a friendship. Let
Him set hand first to that rough stone. And whether
He brings it to completion or succumbs—
Is all one! Let him set his hand to it.
When centuries have run their course and passed,
Then Providence will place a ruler's son,
Like him, upon a throne, like his, once more,
And kindle in her newer favorite
That same idealism. Tell him that
When he becomes a man he should retain   4290
A reverence for the visions of his youth.
And to the deadly insect, Reason, which
Is vaunted as superior, he should
Not open his heart's fragile godly flower—
Nor should he be perplexed when wisdom of
The dust blasphemes idealism, daughter
Of Heaven. I have told him this before—
QUEEN: Marquis, what is this leading to—?
MARQUIS: And say
That I lay human welfare on his soul,
And dying, I demand—demand it of him!   4300
And do so with good right. It would have been
Within my power to bring up new morning
Across these realms. The King had given me
His heart. He has called me his son—I bear
His seals of office, and his Albas are
No more.
                (*He stops and for some minutes silently
                        looks at the Queen.*)

    You weep—O I well recognize
These tears, exalted soul. Joy makes them flow.
But all is over, all is over. Charles
Or I. The choice was quick and terrible.
One of the two was lost, and I intend   4310
To be that one—Yes, rather I than he—
Beyond that do not seek to know.
QUEEN: At last
I now begin to understand you—O,
Unhappy man, what is it you have done?
MARQUIS: Surrendered a few hours of the evening
In order to save a bright summer's day.
I have renounced the King. What can I be
To him in any case? In that hard ground
No roses of my kind can ever bloom—
In my great friend the fate of Europe ripens!   4320
Spain I will relegate to him—Till then
Let it bleed under Philip's hand!—But woe
To me and him if I should rue the choice
Or should perhaps have picked the worse!—No! No!
I know my Carlos—that will never happen—
And *you*, my Queen, shall be my guarantee
For that!

                    (*after a silence*)
            I saw it springing up, that love; I saw
That most unfortunate of passions strike
Its roots within his heart—At that time it
Was still within my power to oppose it.   4330
I did not do so. Not unfortunate
For me, I fostered it. The world may judge
This differently. But I do not regret it.
My heart does not accuse me. I saw life
Where they saw only death—Amid that hopeless flame
I soon discerned the golden ray of hope.
I wished to guide him to the excellent,
I wished to raise him to the highest beauty:

Mortality failed to provide an image,
Speech lacked the words—hence I referred him then   4340
To *this*—To clarify his love to him,
Therein lay my entire achievement.
QUEEN: Marquis,
Your friend fulfilled you so completely that
You quite forgot me over him. Did you
Think in all seriousness that I so lacked
All womanliness, when you made me his angel
And added virtue to his store of weapons?
You must not have considered what a risk
Is taken with our hearts when we ennoble
Passion with a name the like of that.   4350
MARQUIS: For any other woman, not for *one*.
On *one* I take my oath—Or could *you* be
Ashamed of the most noble of desires,
To be creatress of heroic virtue?
What is it to King Philip if his canvas
"Transfiguration" in the Escurial
Inspires the painter standing by it with
Eternity? Does the sweet harmony
That slumbers in the lyre become its buyer's
Who with deaf ears mounts guard above it? He   4360
Has bought the right to shatter it to fragments,
But not the art of charming forth the silver
Tone and melting in the bliss of song.
Truth is available for the wise man,
And Beauty for the feeling heart. You two
Belong to one another. This conviction
No craven prejudice shall overthrow
In me. O promise me to love him always,
And, never tempted by the fear of people
Or false heroics, to a vain denial,   4370
To love him always and unchangingly.
Will you make me this promise?—Queen—Will you
Make me this promise on my hand?

QUEEN: My heart,
   I promise you, alone and ever shall
   Be the judge of my love.
MARQUIS: *(withdraws his hands.)* Now I can die
   In peace—My work is done.
                   (He bows to the Queen and starts
                       to leave.)
QUEEN: *(follows him silently with her eyes.)*
                  You go, Marquis—
   And yet you have not told me when we shall—
   How soon—we meet again.
MARQUIS: *(comes back again, his face averted.)*
                  We certainly
   Shall meet again!
QUEEN: I understand you, Posa—
   I understand you very well—Why did   4380
   You do this to me?
MARQUIS: He or I.
QUEEN: No! No!
   You plunged into this action which you term
   Sublime. Do not deny it. I know you,
   You have been thirsting for it this long time—
   A thousand hearts may break, but what is that
   To you if only you may feed your pride?
   O now—I come to understand you now!
   You only vied for admiration.
MARQUIS: *(struck, to himself)*   No!
   This I was not prepared for—
QUEEN: Marquis!
   Is there no rescue possible?
MARQUIS: None.
QUEEN: None?   4390
   Consider well. Is there none possible?
   Not even, say, through me?
MARQUIS: Not even then.
QUEEN: You only

Half know me—I have courage.

MARQUIS: I know that.

QUEEN: There is no rescue?

MARQUIS: None at all.

QUEEN: (*leaves him and covers her face.*) Then go!
I shall esteem no man again.

MARQUIS: (*throwing himself at her feet in the most
vehement emotion*)

MARQUIS: My Queen!
—My God! but life is beautiful!

> (*He leaps up and walks rapidly away.
> The Queen retires to the inner chamber.*)

SCENE 8

The King's antechamber.
*The Duke of Alba and Domingo are walking back and forth
separately and silently. Count Lerma comes out of the King's
study. Enter presently Don Raimond of Taxis, the Chief
Postmaster.*

LERMA: Has the Marquis not yet been seen?

ALBA: Not yet.

> (*Lerma starts to go back in.*)

TAXIS: (*entering*)
Count Lerma, please announce me to the King.

LERMA: The King may not be seen by anyone.

TAXIS: Say that I *must* speak with him—It concerns   4400
His Majesty most urgently. And hurry.
This will not bear postponing.

> (*Lerma goes into the study.*)

ALBA: (*steps up to the Chief Postmaster.*)
My dear Taxis,
Enure yourself to patience. You will not

Speak with the King—

TAXIS: No? And why not?

ALBA: You should
Have taken the precaution to arrange
Permission with the Cavalier of Posa,
Who has both son and father as his captives.

TAXIS: Of Posa? What? Quite right! That is the man
From whose hand I received this letter—

ALBA: Letter!
What letter?

TAXIS: That I was supposed to forward   4410
To Brussels—

ALBA: (*attentively*)   Brussels?

TAXIS: That I am just bringing
Now to the King—

ALBA: To Brussels! Chaplain, did
You hear that? Brussels!

DOMINGO: (*steps up.*)   This is most suspicious.

TAXIS: How nervously, with what embarrassment
It was entrusted to me!

DOMINGO: Nervously?

ALBA: To whom is it addressed then?

TAXIS: To the Prince
Of Orange-Nassau.

ALBA: William?—Chaplain! This
Is treason.

DOMINGO: What else could it be?—Oh yes,
Beyond a doubt this letter must be taken
Directly to the King. O what a service   4420
On your part, worthy man, to be so strict
About observing service to your King!

TAXIS: I only did my duty, reverend Sir.

ALBA: And you did well.

LERMA: (*comes out of the study. To the Chief Postmaster*)
                    The King will see you now.
                    (*Taxis goes in.*)

And still the Marquis is not here?

DOMINGO: They're looking
Everywhere for him.

ALBA: How odd and strange.
The Prince a prisoner of state, the King'
Himself uncertain as to why.

DOMINGO: He was
Not even here to justify his action?

ALBA: How did the King receive the news?

LERMA: The King   4430
Has not yet said a word.
                    (*A noise in the study.*)

ALBA: What was that? Quiet!

TAXIS: (*coming out of the study*)
Count Lerma!
                    (*Both go in.*)

ALBA: (*to Domingo*)   What is going on here?

DOMINGO: In
That tone of terror! If this intercepted
Letter—? I suspect no good, Duke.

ALBA: He
Calls Lerma! And yet he must know that you
And I are in the anteroom—

DOMINGO: Our times
Are past.

ALBA: Am I not still the same for whom
All doors here used to open? Everything
Is now so changed around me—and so strange—

DOMINGO: (*has gone softly up to the study door and stands
    listening at it.*)
Hark!

ALBA: All is deathly still. One can hear them   4440
Draw breath.

DOMINGO: The double carpet mutes the sound.

ALBA: Away! Someone is coming.

DOMINGO: (*leaves the door.*)   I feel as

Alarmed and solemn as if at this moment
A great fate were to be decided.

(*Enter the Prince of Parma, the Dukes of Feria and Medina
Sidonia with several other grandees.*)

PARMA: May
  The King be seen?
ALBA: No.
PARMA: Who is with him?
FERIA: Marquis
  Of Posa doubtless?
ALBA: They are waiting for him now.
PARMA: This very moment we have just
  Arrived from Saragossa. Terror is
  Abroad through all Madrid—Is it true?
DOMINGO: Yes,
  Unfortunately.
FERIA: It is true then? He was   4450
  Arrested by the Knight of Malta?
ALBA: That
  He was.
PARMA: But why? What happened?
ALBA: Why? Why, not
  A soul knows that except His Majesty
  And Marquis Posa.
PARMA: With no convocation
  Of the Cortes of his own kingdom?
FERIA: Woe
  To any man who took part in this treason.
ALBA: So I cry too.
MEDINA SIDONIA: And I.
THE OTHER GRANDEES: And all of us.
ALBA: Who here will follow me into the study?—
  I'll throw myself at the King's feet.
LERMA: (*rushes out of the study.*) Duke Alba!
DOMINGO: God
  Be praised! At last!

(*Alba hurries in.*)

LERMA: (*breathless, in great excitement*)
                  If the Maltese arrives,   4460
The master is not now alone, he will
Have someone summon him—

DOMINGO: (*to Lerma, as all the others gather around him full
    of curious expectation*)
                      Count, what has happened?
Why, you are as pale as a corpse.

LERMA: (*starts to hurry away.*)   O this
Is devilish!

PARMA AND FERIA: What is? What is?

MEDINA SIDONIA: But the King,
What is he doing in there?

DOMINGO: (*simultaneously*)   Devilish? What?

LERMA: The King
Was weeping.

DOMINGO: Weeping!

ALL OF THEM: (*simultaneously, with startled amazement*)
                    What? The King was weeping!
    (*A bell is heard from within the study. Count Lerma
    hurries in.*)

DOMINGO: (*following him, trying to hold him back*)
Count, one word more—Wait just a—He is gone!
And here we stand stock still and numb with horror.
               (*Enter the Princess of Eboli.*)

EBOLI: (*in haste, frantic*)
Where is the King? Where? I must speak with him.
               (*to Feria*)
Duke you will take me to him.

FERIA: No, the King   4470
Has urgent matters to prevent him. No one
Can be admitted.

EBOLI: Is he signing that
Abominable warrant now? He is
Deceived. And I will prove it to him, that

He is deceived.

DOMINGO: *(gives her a meaningful sign from afar.)*
               Princess of Eboli!

EBOLI: *(walks up to him.)*
Are you here also, Priest? Good! I need you.
You shall corroborate me.
               (She seizes his hand and tries to
               drag him into the study with her.)

DOMINGO: I?—Are you
Out of your mind then, Princess?

FERIA: Stand back there.
The King will not give you a hearing now.

EBOLI: He must give me a hearing. He must hear   4480
The truth—the truth! though he were ten times God!

DOMINGO: Away! You jeopardize all we now have.
Stay here.

EBOLI: Man, tremble at your idol's anger.
For I have nothing left to jeopardize.
    (Just as she is about to enter the study, out rushes Duke
    Alba. His eyes glitter, triumph is in his step. He hurries
    over to Domingo and embraces him.)

ALBA: Have a Te Deum sung in all the churches.
The victory is ours.

DOMINGO: Ours?

ALBA: *(to Domingo and the other grandees)*
               Now go in
There to the lord. You shall hear from me further.   (4487)

ACT V

A room in the royal palace, separated by a wrought-iron door from a large forecourt in which guards are walking up and down.

Carlos is sitting at a table, his head down on his arms as if he were asleep. At the rear of the room are several officers who are locked in with him. The Marquis of Posa enters without being noticed by him; he speaks softly with the officers who immediately withdraw. He steps right up in front of Carlos and contemplates him sadly and in silence for several minutes. Finally he makes a movement that rouses the other from his torpor. Carlos stands up, perceives the Marquis, and shudders from surprise. Then he gazes at him for a time with great wide eyes and runs his hand across his forehead as though he were trying to recall something.

MARQUIS: Charles, it is I.

CARLOS: *(gives him his hand.)* You come to see me even
   Now! That is fine of you.

MARQUIS: I fancied that
   You might have use here for your friend.

CARLOS: Indeed?   4490
   You really thought that? See! That pleases me—
   That pleases me beyond description. Oh!
   I knew you still were fond of me.

MARQUIS: And I
   Have merited it of you, too.

CARLOS: Quite so.

180

O we still understand each other fully.
I like it so. This thoughtfulness, this mildness
Beseems great souls like you and me. Pass over
The fact that one of my demands was quite
Presumptuous and unjust—Must you deny
Me therefore just ones also? Virtue can   4500
Be hard, but cruel never, No, and never
Inhuman.—All that cost you very dearly.
O yes, I think I know quite well how much
Blood was shed by your gentle heart when you
Adorned your victim for the altar.
MARQUIS: Carlos!
How do you mean that?
CARLOS: Now you will yourself
Fulfill the task I should have done and could not—
And *you* will give the Spaniards days of gold
Which they had hoped in vain to get from me.
For me it is all over—and forever.   4510
You realized that—O this dreadful love of mine
Has snatched away beyond recall all of
The early blossoms of my spirit. I
Am dead to *your* great hopes. The King is brought
To you by Providence or Chance—For that
My secret is the price, and it is yours—
Now you are able to become his angel.
For me there is no rescue left—perhaps
For Spain—Ah, there is nothing, nothing here
To blame except my own mad blindness in   4520
Not having realized until today
That you—are just as great as you are gentle.
MARQUIS: No! this, this I did not foresee—did not
Foresee that a friend's magnanimity
Could be more skillful at invention than
My worldly-wise precaution. My whole structure
Collapses—I forgot your heart.
CARLOS: If it had just been possible for you

To save *her* from this fate—my gratitude
To you would have transcended words to tell.   4530
Could I alone not bear it? Did she have
To be a second victim?—But enough!
I will not burden you with a reproach.
What is the Queen to *you? You* do not love
The Queen? Should your strict virtue have to ask
Direction from the petty cares of my
Love? Pardon me—I was unjust.

MARQUIS: You are.
But—not because of this reproach. If I
Deserved this *one,* I would deserve them all—
And I would not be standing *thus* before you.   4540
                    (*He takes out his letter case.*)
Here are some of the letters back again
Which you had given me to keep. Take them.

CARLOS: (*looks with astonishment, now at the letters, now at the
    Marquis.*)
What?

MARQUIS: I am giving them to you again
Because they might be safer now in your
Hands than in mine.

CARLOS: How can that be? But did
The King not get to read them? did he not
So much as get to see them?

MARQUIS: What? *These* letters?

CARLOS: You did not show them all to him?

MARQUIS: Who told
You I had shown him *one?*

CARLOS: (*in extreme astonishment*) But can that be?
Count Lerma.

MARQUIS: *He* told you?—Now everything,   4550
Yes, everything becomes quite clear! Who could
Have foreseen that?—So it was Lerma?—No,
That man has never learned to lie. Quite right,
The other letters are in the King's hands.

CARLOS: *(looks at him for a long time in speechless astonishment.)*
   But then why am I here?
MARQUIS: As a precaution,
   In case you might perhaps be tempted for
   A second time to choose an Eboli
   For confidante—
CARLOS: *(awakening as from a dream)*
           Ah! now at last I see!—
   The light is now beginning—
MARQUIS: *(goes to the door.)*   Who comes here?
              (Enter Duke Alba.)
   *(He approaches the Prince respectfully but keeps his back
   turned on the Marquis throughout the scene.)*
ALBA: Prince, you are free. The King despatched me to   4560
   Announce this to you.
          *(Carlos looks in astonishment at the
          Marquis. All are silent.)*
          Simultaneously,
   Prince, I consider myself fortunate
   To be allowed to be the first to have
   Permission to—
CARLOS: *(observes both with the utmost astonishment.)*
          (After a pause, to the Duke)
          They make me prisoner
   And then declare me free, without my being
   Aware why I was either?
ALBA: By mistake,
   Prince, and as far as I know, one to which
   Some—base deceiver had misled the Monarch.
CARLOS: But it is at the order of the King
   That I am here?
ALBA: Yes, through an error of   4570
   His Majesty.
CARLOS: Well, I am truly sorry
   For that—but if the King has made an error,
   Then it befits the King to come in person

To make that error good.
>   (*He seeks the eyes of the Marquis*
>   *and notices a proud contempt for the Duke.*)
                              They call me here
Don Philip's son. The eyes of slander and
Of curiosity are fixed upon me.
I do not wish to seem to thank his kindness
For what His Majesty did as his duty.
Moreover I am willing to appear
Before the Cortes in tribunal—I   4580
Will not accept my sword from such a hand.

ALBA: The King will not take umbrage at allowing
Your Highness this admissible request
If you will be so kind as to permit
Me to accompany you to him—

CARLOS: I shall
Stay here until the King or his Madrid
Remove me from this prison. Take that answer
To him.
>   (*Alba withdraws. He can be seen standing for a time in
>   the forecourt giving out orders.*)
>   (*Once the Duke has gone, Carlos turns full of expectation
>   and astonishment to the Marquis.*)
                  What does this mean? Explain it to me.
Then are you not the Minister?

MARQUIS: I was,
As you can see.
>   (*going up to him, with great emotion*)
                  O Charles, it has worked out.   4590
It has. It has succeeded. Now it has
Been done. Praised be Almighty God who has
Allowed it to succeed.

CARLOS: Succeed? What? What?
I do not grasp the meaning of your words.

MARQUIS: (*seizes his hand.*)
Charles, you are saved—are free—and I—

(*He checks himself.*)

CARLOS: And you?

MARQUIS: And I—I press you to my bosom now
  For the first time with full and total right;
  I bought it at the cost of everything,
  Of everything that I hold dear—O Charles,
  How sweet, how great this moment is! I am   4600
  Contented with myself.

CARLOS: But what a sudden
  Alteration in your features! I
  Have never seen you thus. More proudly swells
  Your bosom and your glances gleam like fire.

MARQUIS: Charles, we must say farewell. Do not be frightened.
  O be a man. Whatever you may hear,
  Charles, promise me you will not make this parting
  More difficult by an unbridled grief
  Unworthy of great souls—you are about
  To lose me, Charles—for many years—fools say   4610
  Forever.

                (*Carlos draws back his hand, stares at*
                him, and makes no reply.)

              Be a man. I counted much
  On you, nor have I shirked the spending of
  This dread hour with you which is called in terror
  The last—To tell the truth, shall I confess
  It to you, Charles? I had looked forward to it
  With pleasure—Come, let us sit down—I feel
  Dull and exhausted.

        (*He moves closer to Carlos, who is still in a state of dead*
        numbness and who involuntarily lets himself be drawn
        down by him.)

                        Where are all your wits?
  You do not answer me?—I shall be brief.
  The next day after that last time we met
  At the Carthusians' I was summoned to   4620
  The King. With what success you know and all

Madrid knows. But what you do not know is
That someone had betrayed your secret to him,
That letters found in the Queen's jewel-casket
Had testified against you, and that I
Discovered all of this from his own lips,
And that I was—his confidant.

            (*He stops to hear Carlos' answer;*
            the latter maintains his silence.)

                        Yes, Charles,
My own lips broke my loyalty, and I
Myself manipulated the intrigue
That brought about your downfall. But the thing   4630
Had cried too loud. To set you free, it was
Too late. All that was left for me was to
Make sure of his revenge—so I became
Your enemy, to serve you all the better.
—You are not listening?

CARLOS: I am listening. Further.

MARQUIS: To that point I was innocent. But soon
I was betrayed by the unwonted brilliance
Of this new royal favor. As I had
Foreseen, the rumor of it reached your ears.
But I, corrupted by false tenderness,   4640
Blind with the proud illusion of concluding
The scheme without you, went right on concealing
My dangerous secret from our friendship. There
Was my great overhaste! And grievously
I erred. I know that now. My confidence
Was madness. Pardon me—for it was founded
Upon your friendship's everlastingness.

     (*Here he falls silent. Carlos passes from his petrifaction*
     over into the utmost emotion.)

What I had feared, then came to pass. They set
You trembling with concocted perils. First,
The Queen all bathed in blood—the horror of   4650
The echoing palace—and then Lerma's ill-starred

Officiousness—and finally my own
Incomprehensible mad silence, all
Laid siege about your startled heart—you faltered—
You gave me up for lost—And yet, too noble
Yourself to doubt your friend's sincerity,
You decked out his apostasy in greatness,
You now first ventured to declare him faithless
Because you could revere him even faithless.
Deserted by your only friend, you threw   4660
Yourself, unlucky youth, into the arms
Of Princess Eboli, a devil's arms;
For she it was who had betrayed you.
        (Carlos stands up.)   Then
I saw you hurry off. A dark surmise
Fled through my heart. I followed you. Too late.
There at her feet you lay. And the confession
Already was across your lips. For you
There was no rescue—
CARLOS: No! No! She was touched.
You are mistaken. She was surely touched.
MARQUIS: And then across my senses came a darkness!   4670
Nothing—nothing—no way out—no help—
In all the sphere of Nature, none! Despair
Made me a Fury and a beast—I put
The dagger to a woman's heart—But then—
A ray of sunlight fell into my soul.
"What if I could mislead the King? if I
  Could make it look as if I were myself
  The guilty party? Plausible or not!—
  It still would be sufficient for King Philip,
  For it is evil! Good enough! I'll risk it.   4680
  Perhaps a thunderbolt, if it should strike him
  Thus unforeseen, will give the tyrant pause—
  And what more do I want? He'll ponder it,
  And Charles will have gained time to flee to Flanders."
CARLOS: And this—can you have done this?

MARQUIS: I have written
  To William, Prince of Orange, that I loved
  The Queen, and that, by using the suspicion
  Which falsely clung to you, I managed to
  Elude the King's mistrust—that through the Monarch
  Himself I found the means of gaining access   4690
  With freedom to the Queen. I added further
  That I was worried lest I was detected,
  That you, apprised of my infatuation,
  Had hurried to the Princess Eboli,
  Perhaps to have her warn the Queen,—and that
  I had had you arrested here, and now,
  Since all was lost here anyway, was willing
  To flee to Brussels with all haste—This letter—
CARLOS: (interrupts him with terror.)
  You surely did not trust it to the post?
  You know all letters to Brabant and Flanders—   4700
MARQUIS: Are brought directly to the King—As things
  Now stand, it would seem Taxis has already
  Performed his duty.
CARLOS: God! Then I am lost!
MARQUIS: Why *you?*
CARLOS: Unhappy man, and you are lost
  Along with me. My father never will
  Be able to forgive you for this monstrous
  Imposture. No! This he will never pardon.
MARQUIS: Imposture? Why, you are distraught. Reflect.
  Who will tell him it was imposture?
CARLOS: (looks fixedly into his face.)   *Who,*
  You ask? Why, *I* will.
                   (He starts to go.)
MARQUIS: You are mad. Stay here.   4710
CARLOS: Away! In God's name, do not hold me back.
  While I delay here he is hiring his
  Assassins.
MARQUIS: Time is just that much more precious.

We still have much to say to one another.

CARLOS: Before he has discovered—

> (*Again he starts to go. The Marquis takes him by the arm and looks meaningfully at him.*)

MARQUIS: Hear me, Carlos—
Was I so eager or so conscientious
When you were shedding blood for me—a boy?

CARLOS: (*stops before him, touched and full of admiration.*)
O blessed Providence!

MARQUIS: Preserve yourself
For Flanders' sake. The kingship is your calling.
To die for your sake has been mine.

CARLOS: (*steps up to him and takes him by the hand, full of the most profound emotion.*)
                         No! No!   4720
He won't—he cannot possibly refuse!
Can not refuse sublimity like this!—
I'll take you to him. Arm in arm we shall
Walk up to him. And "Father," I will say
To him, "a friend has done this for his friend."
He will be touched. Believe me! he is not
Without humanity, my father. Yes!
Of course he will be touched. His eyes will overflow
With warm tears and he will forgive you and
Forgive me—

> (*A shot is fired through the wrought-iron door. Carlos leaps up.*)
                    Ha! For whom was that intended?   4730

MARQUIS: I think—for me.

> (*He collapses.*)

CARLOS: (*falls on the floor beside him with a cry of grief.*)
O Heaven of Mercy!

MARQUIS: (*his voice breaking*)
O he is quick—the King—I had hoped—just
A little longer—Think of your escape—
You hear?—of your escape—Your mother knows

All this—My life is passing—

(*Carlos remains lying as though dead beside the corpse.*

Enter, after some time, the King, accompanied by the Dukes of Alba, Feria, and Medina Sidonia, the Prince of Parma, Count Lerma, Domingo, and many grandees; he steps back, shocked at this sight.

A general and profound pause. The grandees form a semicircle around the two of them and keep looking back and forth at the King and at his son. The latter is still lying there without any sign of life.—The King gazes at him in pensive silence.)

KING: (*in a kindly tone*)   Your request
Has been accorded, my Infánt. And here
Am I myself with all the grandees of
My kingdom to proclaim you free.

(*Carlos glances up and looks about, like one waking from a dream. His eyes fix now on the King, now on the dead man. He does not answer.*)

                                            Accept
Your sword, which I return. We moved too fast.

(*He approaches him, gives him his hand,
                    and helps him up.*)

My son is not in his right place. Stand up.   4740
Come to your father's arms.

CARLOS: (*without awareness receives the King's arms—then suddenly recalls, stops, and looks about more carefully.*)

                                    The smell of you
Is murder. I can't put my arms around you.

(*He thrusts him back. All the
                    grandees are in commotion.*)

No! Do not stand there so amazed! What have
I done so terrible? Laid hands upon
The Heaven's Anointed? You need have no fear.
I shall not lay a hand on him. Do you
Not see the brand upon his forehead? God
Has marked him.

KING: *(starting swiftly to leave)*

                      Follow me, all you grandees.

CARLOS: Where to? Not from this spot, Sire—

    (He holds him with both hands by force and with one hand
    manages to seize the sword which the King has brought.
    It comes out of its sheath.)

KING: You would draw

The sword against your father?

ALL GRANDEES PRESENT: *(drawing theirs)* Regicide!   4750

CARLOS: *(holding the King firmly by one hand and with the*
    naked sword in the other)

Put up your swords. What do you want? Do you

Think I am mad? Oh no, I am not mad.

But if I were, you did unwisely in

Reminding me that his life hovers on

My sword-point. I would beg you to hold off.

For constitutions such as mine want to

Be humored—so stand back. The thing I have

To settle with this king no wise concerns

Your oaths of fealty. Just look, however,

At how his fingers bleed! Look close at him!   4760

You see? O then look here too—*This* is his

Work, this great artist's!

KING: *(to the grandees, who are trying in their concern to close*
    up around him)

                    Step back, all of you.

What are you trembling at?—Are we not father

And son? I will, however, wait and see

To what disgraceful action Nature—

CARLOS: Nature?

I know of none. Now Murder is the watchword.

The bonds of human kind are cleft in twain.

You have torn them yourself, Sire, in your kingdoms.

Am I to honor what you mock?—O see!

See here! No murder has yet been committed   4770

Before today—Is there no God? Are kings

Allowed to house this way in His creation?
I ask again: Is there no God? As long as mothers
Have borne, there has been one and only one
Who died so undeservedly—And do
You know *what* you have done? No, he does not,
He does not know that he has stolen from
This world a life that was more noble, more
Important, and more dear than he and all
His century.

KING: (*in a lenient tone*)
             If I have been too sudden,   4780
Does it beseem you now to call me to
Account *for* whom I was so?

CARLOS: What? Can it
Be possible? You have not guessed yet what
This dead man was to me?—O tell him then—
Help his Omniscience solve the weighty riddle.
The dead man was my friend—And would you like
To know what he died for? He died for me.

KING: Ha! my presentiment!

CARLOS: Forgive me, you
Who lie here bleeding, for profaning it*
Before such ears! But this great connoisseur   4790
Of men can drop for shame to think a youth's
Astuteness has outwitted his grey wisdom.
Sire, we were brothers! brothers by a bond
More noble than the one that Nature forges.
His noble life was love. And love for me
Was his great noble death. And he was *mine*
While you were touting his respect for you
And while his nimble fluency of speech
Was playing with your proud colossus-mind.
You fancied you had mastered him—and were   4800

---

* Only by reference to the prose version of *Don Carlos* do we discover that
the word *it* (es) refers to *our secret* (unser Geheimnis). The antecedent got
lost in the process of textual revision.

The docile instrument of his high plans.
My own imprisonment was the precise
Contrivance of his friendship. And the letter
To Orange he composed to rescue me—
My God! It was the first lie in his life!
To rescue me he threw himself at that
Death which he suffered. You may have accorded him
Your favor—but he died for me. Your heart
And friendship you had forced upon him, but
Your sceptre was the plaything of his hands;   4810
He threw it down and died for me!
    (*The King stands motionless, his gaze fixed on the floor.*
    All the grandees stand abashed and fearful around him.)
                                    And was
It possible? You could lend credence to
That clumsy lie? What scorn he must have had
For you when undertaking to achieve
His ends with you by that crude artifice!
And you presumed to court his friendship, yet
You were inadequate in that slight test.
O no—no, that was not for you. That was
No man for you! He realized that fully
When he rejected you and all crowned heads.   4820
That subtle instrument was shattered in
Your iron hand. You could do nothing else
But murder him.
ALBA: (*has up till now not taken his eyes off the King and has*
    been observing his movements with perceptible disquiet as
    they work in his face. Now he timidly approaches him.)
                  Sire—not this deathly silence.
Do look around you. Speak to us.
CARLOS: He did
Not feel indifference toward you. You long
Had had his sympathetic interest.
Perhaps he even would have made you happy.
His heart was rich enough to satisfy

You from his superfluity. The splinters
From his mind would have made a god of you.   4830
You have robbed yourself—
What will you offer to replace a soul
The like of this?

> (*A profound silence. Many of the grandees look away or
> cover their faces with their mantles.*)

O you who stand assembled here all mute with horror
And with astonishment—do not condemn
The young man who has used such language to
His father and his King—Behold this sight!
He gave his life for me! Do you have tears?
Does blood, not molten brass, flow in your veins?
Behold, and then do not condemn me!

> (*He turns to the King with more composure
> and moderation.*)

You   4840

Perhaps are waiting now to see how this unnatural story
Will end?—Here is my sword. You are my King
Once more. Do you think that I tremble at
Your vengeance? Murder me just as you had
This noblest of all human beings murdered.
My life is forfeit. That I know. What is
Life to me now? I here renounce all that
This world may have in store for me. Go find
Yourself a son among unknowns and strangers.
Here lie my kingdoms—

> (*He sinks down beside the corpse and takes no further part
> in what follows.*
>
> *Meanwhile a confused din of voices and a thronging of
> many people is heard in the distance. Around the King
> there is profound silence. His eyes pass over the whole
> group, but no one meets his glances.*)

KING: Well? Will no one answer?—   4850
You all stand with your looks cast to the ground—

Each face concealed!—My sentence has been passed.
I read it as it is proclaimed in these
Mute glances here. My subjects have passed judgment on me.
  (*Silence as before.—The tumult comes closer and becomes
  louder. A murmur runs through the group of grandees.
  They make perplexed signs to each other; Count Lerma
  finally nudges the Duke of Alba gently.*)
LERMA: This is indeed a storm.
ALBA: (*softly*)   I fear it is.
LERMA: They're coming. Forcing their way up.
          (*Enter an officer of the bodyguard.*)
THE OFFICER: (*urgently*)   Rebellion!
  Where is the King?
    (*He works his way through the crowd and presses forward
    until he comes to the King.*)
                  Sire, all Madrid is up
In arms! The raging soldiers and the mob
Are ringed about the palace by the thousands.
Prince Carlos, rumor claims, has been arrested,   4860
His life imperiled, and the people want
To see him in the flesh or they will have
All of Madrid in flames.
ALL THE GRANDEES: (*in commotion*)   Help! Save the King!
  O save the King!
ALBA: (*to the King, who is standing quiet and motionless*)
                  Sire, there is danger—Flee!—
We do not know yet who it is that gives
This mob its weapons—
KING: (*rouses from his stupor, braces himself, and steps with
    majesty among them.*)
                  Is my throne
Still standing? Am I still this country's King?—
No. That I am no longer. By a boy
Made soft, these cowards whimper. They are waiting
For nothing but the watchword to desert me.   4870

I find myself betrayed by rebels.

ALBA: Sire,
What a ghastly fancy!

KING: Over there!
Go cast yourselves down over there! Before
The young king in his springtime cast yourselves
Down—I am nothing any more—a helpless
Old man!

ALBA: Have things gone that far!—Spaniards!
   (*They all press around the King and kneel before him
   with swords drawn. Carlos remains alone and deserted by
   all, beside the corpse.*)

KING: (*tears off his mantle and throws it away.*)
                                        Clothe

Him in the royal robe—and carry him
Upon my trampled corpse—
         (*He collapses in the arms of Alba
         and Lerma.*)

LERMA: Help! Help! My God!

FERIA: What a mischance!

LERMA: He is out of his mind—

ALBA: (*leaves the King in the hands of Lerma and Feria.*)
Get him to bed. And I meanwhile will give   4880
Peace to Madrid.
            (*Exit.*)
   (*The King is carried off, and all the grandees accompany
   him.*)
   (*Carlos remains behind, alone, with the corpse. Enter after
   a few minutes Luis Mercado, who looks about timidly
   and stands for a time in silence behind the Prince, who
   does not notice him.*)

MERCADO: I bring
A message from Her Majesty the Queen.
        (*Carlos looks away again and gives
        him no reply.*)

Mercado is my name—I am Physician
Attendant to Her Majesty—and here
Are my credentials.
　　　　　(*He shows the Prince a signet ring.—*
　　　　　The latter persists in his silence.)
　　　　　　　　It is the Queen's wish
To see you yet today—affairs of some
Importance—
CARLOS:　　　　Nothing in this world
Is of importance now to me.
MERCADO:　　　　　　　She said
The Marquis Posa left a message—
CARLOS: (*stands up quickly.*)　　What?
Directly.
　　　　　(*He starts to go with him.*)
MERCADO:　No! Not now, Prince. You must wait　　4890
For nightfall. Every avenue of access
Is manned and all the guards are doubled there.
It is impossible to set a foot
In that wing of the palace unobserved.
You would put everything in jeopardy—
CARLOS: But—
MERCADO:　　Only one expedient, Prince, remains.
The Queen has thought it up. She now proposes
It to you. It is daring, though, and odd,
And quite fantastic.
CARLOS:　　　　Namely?
MERCADO:　　　　　　As you know,
There long has been a legend current that　　4900
At midnight in the vaulted corridors
About the royal palace Emperor Charles's
Departed spirit walks, garbed as a monk.
The common folk believe this rumor and
The guards take up their posts with terror there.
If you are of a mind to take

Advantage of that same disguise, you can
Pass freely and unharmed through all the guards
Right to the Queen's apartment, which this key
Will then unlock. The sacred figure will protect you   4910
From all attack. But your decision must
Be made, Prince, instantly. The necessary
Accouterments and mask you will discover
Laid ready in your chamber. I must hurry now to bring
Her Majesty your answer.

CARLOS: And the time?

MERCADO: The time is midnight.

CARLOS: Tell her that she may
Expect me.

(Exit Mercado.)
(Enter Count Lerma.)

LERMA: Prince, make your escape at once.
The King is in a rage against you. Some
Design upon your liberty—if not
Upon your life. Ask me no further. I   4920
Have slipped away to warn you. Flee without
Delay.

CARLOS: I am in the Almighty's hands.

LERMA: But as the Queen just now impressed upon me,
You are to leave Madrid and flee to Brussels
This very day. Do not, do not postpone it!
The insurrection favors your escape.
It was with that intention that the Queen
Had instigated it. Now they will not
Be so bold as to move by force against you.
At the Carthusian monastery you   4930
Will find the post awaiting you, and here
Are weapons if you should have need—

(He gives him a dagger and pocket pistols.)

CARLOS: Thanks, thanks,
Count Lerma!

LERMA: What you told us here today
  Touched me profoundly. No friend loves in that
  Way any more. All patriots lament
  For you. More I may not say now.
CARLOS: Count Lerma! The deceased spoke of you as
  A noble man.
LERMA: Prince, once again I say:
  Prosperous be your journey! Better times will come;
  But I shall then no longer be alive.   4940
  Receive my homage now.
                    (*He falls on one knee before him.*)
CARLOS: (*attempts to prevent him. Deeply moved*)
                    O do not do
  This—Do not do this, Count—You move me—I am
  Unwilling to be weak—
LERMA: (*kisses his hand with emotion.*)
                    My children's King!
  My children, they will have the privilege
  Of dying for you. I can not. But in my children
  Remember me—Return in peace to Spain.
  And may you be a human being on
  King Philip's throne. You also have learned how
  To suffer. Undertake no deed of blood against
  Your father! No, my Prince, no deed of blood!   4950
  Philip the Second forced your father's father
  To abdicate his throne—And now today
  This Philip trembles at the sight of his
  Own son. Remember *that,* my Prince,—and so
  May Heaven be your guide upon your way!
                    (*Exit rapidly.*)
  (*Carlos is on the point of hurrying away in a different
  direction but turns suddenly around, throws himself
  down before the corpse, and clasps it once more in his
  arms. Then he swiftly quits the room.*)

SCENE 2

The King's antechamber.
A throng of many grandees. It is evening and lights are being
lighted. Enter the Duke of Alba in conversation with the Duke
of Feria.

ALBA: The town is calm. How did you leave the King?
FERIA: In the most dreadful state of mind. He has
  Locked himself in his room. No matter what
  May happen, he will not admit a soul
  Into his presence. The Marquis' betrayal   4960
  Has all at once transformed his entire nature.
  We do not recognize him any more.
ALBA: I have to see him. This time I can not
  Spare him. A new discovery of importance
  Which has just now been made—
FERIA: A new discovery?
ALBA: My guards' attention has been caught by some
  Carthusian monk who secretly had stolen
  Into the Prince's room and was inquiring
  With curiosity into the death
  Of Marquis Posa. They arrested him.   4970
  They questioned him. The fear of death extorted
  Confession from him that he had upon
  His person papers of great value which
  The dead man had entrusted to his charge
  To be delivered in the Prince's hands—
  In case he should not reappear before
  The set of sun.
FERIA: So? Well?
ALBA: The letters say
  That Carlos is to leave Madrid between
  Midnight and morning.
FERIA: What?

ALBA: And that a ship
  Is lying ready at Cadiz to sail   4980
  With him to Vlissingen—that the States of
  The Netherlands are waiting only for
  His coming to throw off the Spanish chains.
FERIA: Ha! What is this?
ALBA: Another letter
  Reports a fleet of Suleiman's as having
  Already started out from Rhodes—this in
  Accordance with a prearranged alliance—
  For an attack against the King of Spain
  In the Mediterranean Sea.
FERIA: Can that
  Be possible?
ALBA: These letters further list   4990
  The journeys that this Knight of Malta made
  Through Europe recently. His goal was nothing
  Less than the arming of all northern powers
  For Flemish freedom.
FERIA: He was of that sort!
ALBA: These letters finally are followed by
  A detailed outline of the entire war
  Which is to separate the Netherlands
  Forever from the Spanish monarchy,
  With nothing, nothing overlooked, strength and
  Resistance calculated, all the country's   5000
  Resources accurately indicated,
  All maxims to be followed, treaties to
  Be made. The sketch is devilish,
  But truly—god-like.
FERIA: What a devious traitor!
ALBA: This letter makes the further mention of
  A secret conversation which the Prince
  Is to arrange the night before his flight
  Between him and his mother.
FERIA: What? Why, that's

Today.

ALBA: This very midnight. I have issued
Instructions covering that point already.   5010
You see that this is urgent. Not a minute
Is to be lost—So open up the door
Of the King's room.

FERIA: No! Entrance is forbidden.

ALBA: Then I shall open it myself—The mounting
Danger justifies this boldness—

         (As he is walking toward the door,
           it is opened and the King steps forth.)

FERIA: Ha!
The King in person!

    (Enter the King.—At the sight of him they are all startled,
    fall back, and reverently allow him to pass through their
    midst. He comes out in a state of waking dream, like a
    sleep-walker.—His attire and figure still show evidence of
    the disrangement occasioned by his previous fainting
    spell. With slow step he walks past the grandees present,
    looks fixedly at each without perceiving a single one of
    them. Finally he halts, with eyes cast to the floor, until
    gradually the emotions of his mind acquire the sound of
    words.)

KING: Give me back this dead
Man. I must have him back.

DOMINGO: *(softly to the Duke of Alba)* Go speak to him.

KING: *(as before)*
He took me to be small and died. I have
To have him back. He has to think of me
A different way.

ALBA: *(approaches with fear.)*
         Sire—

KING: Who speaks here?
    (He casts a long glance around the whole
          group.)

               Is it   5020

Forgotten who I am? Why are you not
Down on your knees before me, creature? I
Am still the King. I want to see submission.
Does everyone shirk deference because
One man despised me?
ALBA: Think no more of him,
My King! Another enemy, more drastic
Than he, stands in your kingdom's heart—
FERIA: Prince Carlos—
KING: He had a friend who died for him—for him!
With me he could have shared a royal kingdom!
How he looked down on me!—One does not look   5030
That haughtily down from the thrones of monarchs.
Was it not obvious how well he understood
The value of a conquest such as *that?*
What he had lost, his grief acknowledged. No
One mourns like that for any transitory thing—
Would he were still alive! I'd give the Indies for it.
O woe-begone omnipotence that can
Not even stretch its arm forth into graves
To right a little hastiness with human
Life. Dead men resurrect no more. Who can   5040
Tell me that I am happy? In the grave
Dwells one man who withheld respect from me.
What do I care about those still alive?
A spirit, *one* free man rose up in all
This century—just one—and he despised me
And died.
ALBA: Then we have lived in vain!—Let us
Go to our graves, then, Spaniards. Even in
His death this man is robbing us of our
King's heart!
KING: (*He sits down and props his head on his arm.*)
                If he had died like that for *me!*
I held him dear, I held him very dear.
He was as dear to me as any son.

In that youth rose for me a new and fairer
Morning. Who knows what I held in store
For him? And he was my first love. All Europe
May curse me! Let all Europe curse me then.
I did deserve the gratitude of this
Man.
DOMINGO: By what magic—
KING: And this sacrifice
Was made for whom? That boy, my son? No, never.
That I do not believe. A Posa does
Not perish for a boy. Nor does mere friendship's   5060
Flame fill a Posa's heart. That beat for all
Humanity. No, his affection was
The world with all its coming generations.
And to give them their due he found a throne—
Which he abandons now? Could Posa ever
Forgive himself this treachery to his
Humanity? No. I know him too well.
He did not sacrifice his Philip for
His Carlos, but the old man for the young
One, his disciple; for the father's sunset   5070
No longer makes the day's work worth the effort.
That is saved for the present sunrise of the son—
O it is quite clear! He was waiting for my death.
ALBA: Read the confirmation in these letters.
KING: (rising)
It may be that he has miscalculated.
I still exist. For which I thank thee, Nature.
I still feel youthful strength in all my sinews.
And I shall make a laughing-stock of him.
His virtue shall have been a dreamer's phantom.
Let him have died a fool. And let his fall   5080
Drag down his friend and all his century!
Let's see how well they get along without me.
The world belongs to me yet for my evening,
And I shall use that evening so that for

Ten human ages after me no sower
Shall reap again this charred and fire-swept field.
He sacrificed me to humanity,
His idol; let humanity atone
For him!—And now—I will start with his puppet.
                    (*to the Duke of Alba*)
What was it that you said concerning the Infante?   5090
Say that again. What do these letters tell me?

ALBA: (These letters, Sire, contain the legacy
Of Marquis Posa to Prince Charles.

KING: (*runs through the papers, during which time he is sharply
    observed by all present. After he has read for a time, he
    lays them aside and paces silently through the room.*)
                              Go summon
The Cardinal Inquisitor. Say that
I beg him to grant me an hour's time.
    (*One of the grandees goes out. The King takes up the
    papers again, reads further, and again puts them aside.*)
Tonight, then?

TAXIS: At the stroke of two the post
Will stop at the Carthusian monastery.

ALBA: And persons whom I had sent out observed
Assorted lots of luggage, each one with
The royal arms stamped on it, being carried   5100
Out toward the monastery.

FERIA: Large sums also
Are said to have been raised in the Queen's name
Among the Moorish bankers for redemption
In cash at Brussels.

KING: Where was the Infante
Last seen?

ALBA: Beside the Knight of Malta's corpse.

KING: Is there
Still light in the Queen's room?

ALBA: There all is quiet.
She has dismissed her chamber-women too

Somewhat more early than her custom is.
The Duchess of Arcos who was the last
To quit her room, left her already in　　　　　　5110
Deep sleep.

　　　(*Enter an Officer of the bodyguard. He draws the Duke of
　　　Feria aside and talks softly with him. The latter turns in
　　　surprise to the Duke of Alba. Others gather around and
　　　a murmur of voices grows louder.*)

FERIA: ⎫
TAXIS: ⎬ (*simultaneously*)　How strange!
DOMINGO: ⎭

KING:　　　　　　　　　What is the matter?

FERIA:　Sire, a report which it is difficult
To credit—

DOMINGO:　Sire, two Switzers who have just
Come off their posts report—It is absurd
Repeating what they say.

KING:　　　　　　　　What *do* they say?

ALBA:　They say that in the left wing of the palace
The spectre of the Emperor was observed
To cross their path with firm and solemn tread and pass
Beyond them out of sight. This same report
Is reaffirmed by all the guards who mount　　　　5120
Their posts through that pavilion, and they add
The apparition disappeared within
The Queen's apartments.

KING:　　　　　　　　In what form did he
Appear?

OFFICER:　In that same garb that he wore as
A monk at San Geronimo de Just
In those last days of his existence.

KING:　　　　　　　　As
A monk? And had the guards then been acquainted
With him while he was still alive? How else
Could they have known it was the Emperor?

OFFICER:　　　　　　　　That

It must have been the Emperor was proved by   5130
The sceptre that he carried in his hands.
DOMINGO: Besides, he often has, as rumor claims,
Been seen in that form.
KING: No one spoke to him?
OFFICER: No one had the temerity to do so.
The guardsmen said their prayers and reverently
Let him pass through their midst.
KING: And in the Queen's apartments
The apparition vanished from your sight?
OFFICER: In the Queen's anteroom.
                        (General silence.)
KING: (turns around suddenly.)   What do you say?
ALBA: Sire, we are mute.
KING: (after some reflection, to the Officer)
                        Have my whole guard report
In arms and take positions blocking all   5140
Approaches to that wing. I eagerly
Desire to have a word with this ghost.
                        (Exit the Officer.
                        Enter a Page.)
PAGE: Sire,
The Cardinal Inquisitor.
KING: (to those present)   Leave us.
    (Enter the Cardinal Grand Inquisitor, ninety years of age
    and blind, leaning on a staff, and led by two Dominicans.
    As he passes among them, all the grandees fall upon their
    knees before him and touch the hem of his garment. He
    extends his blessing to them. They all withdraw.—A long
    silence.)
GRAND INQUISITOR: Do I
Now stand before the King?
KING: Yes.
GRAND INQUISITOR: I had not
Expected to again.
KING: I now renew

A scene of former years. Infante Philip
Seeks counsel from his teacher.
GRAND INQUISITOR: Counsel never
Was needed by my pupil Charles, your father.
KING: He was that much more fortunate. I have
Committed murder, Cardinal. No peace—   5150
GRAND INQUISITOR: Why did you commit this murder?
KING: A
Betrayal without parallel—
GRAND INQUISITOR: I know it.
KING: What do you know? Through whom? Since when?
GRAND INQUISITOR: For years,
What *you* have known since sunset.
KING: (*surprised*)   What? You had
Already known about this man?
GRAND INQUISITOR: His life
Lies opened and concluded in the holy
Record-ledgers of the Santa Casa.
KING: And he walked free?
GRAND INQUISITOR: The cord on which he fluttered
Was long, but still unbreakable.
KING: But he
Had been beyond my kingdom's boundaries.   5160
GRAND INQUISITOR: Wherever he might be, there I was also.
KING: (*walking impatiently back and forth*)
It was known in whose hands I was—Why then was there
Delay in warning me?
GRAND INQUISITOR: That question I
Turn back upon you—Why did *you* not ask
When you threw yourself into this man's arms?
You knew him well! One glance would have unmasked
The heretic—Who authorized you to
Deprive the Holy Office of this victim?
Is this the way to trifle with us? If
The Crown stoops to concealment—reaches understandings 5170

Behind our backs with our worst enemies,
Where will we be? If one man is shown mercy,
By what right can a hundred thousand then
Be sacrificed?

KING: He has been sacrificed.

GRAND INQUISITOR: No! He was murdered—wantonly! inglori-
The blood that should have flowed for us in glory   [ously!—
Was shed by an assassin's hand. The man
Was ours—Who authorized *you* to lay hands
Upon the Order's sacred property?
To die for us was his excuse for living.   5180
God granted him unto this epoch's need
To make of swaggering Reason an example
By formal degradation of his mind.
That was my well considered plan. And now
It lies wiped out, my work of many years!
We have been cheated, robbed, and you have nothing
But bloody hands.

KING: My passion swept me on.
Forgive me.

GRAND INQUISITOR: Passion!—Does this answer come
From the Infante Philip? Am I all
Alone in having reached old age?—Your passion!   5190
             (*with indignant shaking of the head*)
Give liberty of conscience in your realms
When you are walking in your chains.

KING: In matters
Like these I am a novice still. Have patience
With me.

GRAND INQUISITOR: No! No! I am not satisfied
With you.—To think that you would slander your
Whole course of regency this way! Where was
That Philip at the time, whose steadfast soul,
Unchanging like the pivot-star in heaven,
Turns everlastingly about itself? Was all

Past time entirely sunk behind you? Was 5200
The world no more the same that moment when
You offered him your hand? Was poison no
More poison? Had the barrier-wall collapsed
Between all good and evil, true and false?
What is resolve, or what is constancy,
Or loyalty of men, if in a tepid
Minute's space a rule of sixty years
Will vanish like a woman's whim?

KING: I looked into his eyes—Allow therefore
For my relapse into mortality. 5210
The world has that one avenue the less
Into your heart. The vision of your eyes is quenched.

GRAND INQUISITOR: What was this man supposed to be to you?
What new things could he possibly have had
To show you for which you were not prepared?
Do you know fever-dreams and innovation
So little? Did the loud-mouth talk of world-
Improvers ring so strange upon your ears?
For if the edifice of your convictions
Will topple at mere words—with what face, may 5220
I ask, did you sign execution warrants
For all those hundred thousand feeble souls
Who have gone to the stake for nothing worse?

KING: I yearned for just one human being. These
Domingos—

GRAND INQUISITOR: Why a human being? Human
Beings are mere digits, nothing more,
To you. Must I hear my grey student say
His lesson on Essentials of the Art
Of Ruling? Let the god of earth unlearn
The need of what can be refused to him— 5230
If *you* go whimpering for sympathy,
Have you not then confessed yourself the world's
Own kind? And what rights, I should like to know,

    Do you have claim to over your own kind?
KING: (*throws himself into the armchair.*)
    I am a little man, I realize—
    You ask the creature for what the Creator
    Alone can do.
GRAND INQUISITOR: No, Sire, I am not fooled.
    I see through you—You wanted to
    Escape from us. The Order's heavy chains
    Oppressed you; you intended to   5240
    Be free and independent.
                  (*He stops. The King is silent.*)
                          We have been
    Avenged, however—Thank the Church who is
    Content to punish as a mother. That
    Choice which you blindly were allowed to make
    Was your chastisement. You have been instructed.
    And now come back to us—If I did not
    Stand now before you—by the living God!
    You would have stood before me thus tomorrow.
KING: Priest, watch your tongue! I will not have myself
    Addressed in such a tone.
GRAND INQUISITOR: Then why have you called up   5250
    The shade of Samuel?—Two kings have I
    Placed on the Spanish throne, and I had hoped
    To leave a firmly founded work behind me.
    I see my life's fruits lost. Don Philip shatters
    My edifice himself. And now, Sire—Why
    Have I been summoned? What am I supposed
    To do here?—I am quite unwilling to
    Repeat this visit.
KING: One task yet remains undone,
    The last—and then you may depart in peace.
    Let past events be of the past, let there   5260
    Be peace betwen us—We are reconciled?
GRAND INQUISITOR: If Philip humbly bows.

KING: (*after a pause*)   My son is planning
  Rebellion.
GRAND INQUISITOR: What have you decided?
KING: Nothing—
  Or everything.
GRAND INQUISITOR: And what is everything
  In this case?
KING: I will let him flee,
  Or else put him to death.
GRAND INQUISITOR: Well, Sire?
KING: Can you create a new religion which
  Supports the bloody murder of a son?
GRAND INQUISITOR: To expiate eternal Righteousness
  God's own son died upon the cross.
KING: Do you   5270
  Agree to sow this notion through all Europe?
GRAND INQUISITOR: As far as they adore the Cross.
KING: I outrage
  Nature too—Will you put silence on
  That mighty voice as well?
GRAND INQUISITOR: Before the Faith
  No voice of Nature has validity.
KING: I place my judge's office in your hands—
  Can I withdraw entirely?
GRAND INQUISITOR: Trust it wholly
  To me.
KING: This is my only son—What have
  I labored for?
GRAND INQUISITOR: For moldering death, before
  Such freedom.
KING: (*rising*)   We are in agreement. Come.   5280
GRAND INQUISITOR: Where?
KING: To receive the victim from my hands.
                    (*He leads him away.*)

SCENE 3

The Queen's apartments.
Enter Carlos in monk's habit, on his face a mask which he is
just taking off, and a naked sword under his arm. It is very
dark. He approaches a door which is opened. From it emerges
the Queen in night garments and carrying a burning candle.
Carlos falls on one knee before her.

CARLOS: Elizabeth!
QUEEN: (*resting her gaze with quiet sadness upon his face*)
                    Is this the way we meet
  Again!
CARLOS: This is the way we meet again!
                    (*Silence.*)
QUEEN: (*tries to get possession of herself.*)   Arise.
  We shall not make each other weak, Charles. Not
  By helpless tears will that great dead man best
  Be honored. Tears may flow for lesser sorrows!—
  He sacrificed himself for *you!* and at
  The cost of his most precious life
  He has redeemed and purchased yours—And shall that blood   5290
  Have been poured forth for an illusion?—Carlos!
  I was myself your guarantee to him,
  And on the warrant of that pledge he went
  Away more joyously. Will you now make
  A liar out of me?
CARLOS: (*impassioned*)   I shall erect
  A monument to him such as no king
  Has ever known—A Paradise shall bloom
  Above his ashes!
QUEEN: Thus I wished to have you!
  That was the lofty meaning of his death!
  He chose me to be the executrix
  Of his last will. I warn you that I shall   5300

Hold you to the fulfillment of that vow.
—And still another legacy that man
About to die placed in my hand—I gave him
My word—and—why should I not speak of it?
He gave his Charles into my keeping—I
Defy appearances—I shall not tremble
At people any more, I will be bold
Now, like a friend. My heart shall speak. Did he
Call our love virtue? I believe him, and
My heart no longer—

CARLOS: Do not finish, Queen—   5310
I have lain in a long, oppressive dream.
I loved—but now I have awakened. Let
The past be past and done. Your letters I
Herewith return. Destroy mine also. Fear
No further outbursts of my passion. That
Is done. A purer fire has clarified
My being, and my passion dwells in graves among
The dead. No mortal appetites divide
My bosom any longer.
                (after a silence, taking her hand)
                        I have come   5320
To say farewell—I realize at last
There is a higher good, a good more worthy
Of seeking, Mother, than possessing you—
A brief night has lent wings to my years' lanquid
Flight and ripened me to manhood early.
I have no further task in this life but
To keep the memory of him! My harvests
Have all been garnered—
                *(He approaches the Queen, who
                covers her face.)*
                        Mother, have you nothing
To say to me?
QUEEN: Pay no heed to my tears,
Charles,—I can not do otherwise than weep—

Believe me though in saying I admire you.　　　5330
CARLOS: You were the only confidante of our
Alliance—By *that* name you shall remain
The dearest thing in all the world to me.
I can as little grant my friendship to you
As I could yesterday bestow my love
On any other woman—Holy shall
The royal widow be to me however,
If Providence conducts me to this throne.
　　　(Unnoticed in the background appears the King, accom-
　　　　panied by the Grand Inquisitor and his grandees.)
I leave Spain now and shall not see my father
Again—no, never in this life again.　　　　　5340
I feel no more affection for him. Nature
Has withered in my bosom.—Be his spouse
Once more. His son is lost to him. Go back
And reassume your duties. I now hasten
To rescue my oppressed and harried people
Who live beneath his tyrant's hand. Madrid
Shall see me as a king or never see me.
And now a final time: Farewell!
　　　　　　　(He kisses her.)
QUEEN:　　　　　　　　O Charles!
What have you made of me?—I may not venture
To rise to such a height of manly greatness;　　5350
But I can comprehend you and admire.
CARLOS: Am I not strong, Elizabeth? I hold
You in my arms now and I do not falter.
Yesterday the terrors of close death
Would not have torn me from this spot.
　　　　　　　(He releases her.)
　　　　　　　　　　　　But that
Is over. Every fate of mortal man
I now defy. I held you in my arms
And did not falter.—Quiet! Did you not
Hear something?

(A clock strikes.)

QUEEN: Nothing but that dreadful clock
That strikes the hour for us to part.

CARLOS: Good night, then, Mother   5360
From Ghent you will have my first letter, and
It will proclaim the secret of our high
Collaboration. I go now to challenge
Don Philip in the open field of battle.
Henceforth I want no secret matters held
Between us. *You* no longer need to flee
From the world's eye—Let this have been my last
Deceit.

            *(He is about to reach for the mask.
              The King intervenes.)*

KING: It is your last one.

                    (The Queen faints.)

CARLOS: *(runs to her and takes her in his arms.)*
                        Is she dead?
O earth and heaven!

KING: *(coldly and quietly to the Grand Inquisitor)*
                    Cardinal! I have
Done what my part required. Do your part now.   5370

            (Exit.)

            T H E   E N D